† THE UPWARD ARROW

†

THE UPWARD ARROW

A Way of Holiness for Every Home

FR. COLUM POWER

Scepter

Praise for

THE UPWARD ARROW

I love Fr. Colum! Of the dozens of priests whom I've known over the years, there are few I love more. There are many reasons for this. One is his ability to spin a good yarn, or what he might call the gift of the blarney or the gift of the gab. Another is his gift as a very fine writer of poetic prose. Yet another is his lived love for the Lord. All three of these things that I love about Fr. Colum are present in this book. I can think of no better reason to read it and learn from it, not least because it will help us to live the love for the Lord.

— **Joseph Pearce**, Director of the Center for Faith and Culture at Aquinas College, co-editor of the *St. Austin Review*, and author of over thirty books including *Benedict XVI: Defender of the Faith, and Literature: What Every Catholic Should Know.*

Fr. Colum Power, with his very Irish gift for telling a tale, has given us a remarkable book, full of powerful stories drawn from daily life, history, and Scripture. Vigorous, funny, and overflowing with unflinching pastoral wisdom, *The Upward Arrow* begins as a son's tribute to his parents' marriage and becomes not only a celebration of the Christian family but also a road map for Christian life in our own difficult times.

— **Fr. John Wauck**, professor of Literature and Communication of the Faith at The Pontifical University of the Holy Cross, Rome.

The Upward Arrow directs our gaze to our proper target: the joy of Christ that reaches us through the messiness of everyday life. The commitment of spouses to one another and to their children truly becomes a ladder that draws us upward by pulling us out of ourselves in love. Fr. Colum Power uses his exceptional wisdom and wit to enliven our imaginations with stories of the Lord's patient providence that brings us to holiness in and through our homes.

— **Dr. R. Jared Staudt**, visiting associate professor at the Augustine Institute and author of *How the Eucharist Can Save Civilization.*

"Man has places in his heart which do not yet exist," said the great Catholic writer Léon Bloy, "and into them enters suffering, in order that they may have existence." With unflinching attention to the inevitable heartbreaks that mark every marriage worth its salt, Fr. Colum Power brings his wit and wisdom to make these wounds into spacious rooms of real wisdom. May many marriages be mended through this book, and may Our Father Who Art in Heaven "turn the heart of the fathers to the children, and the heart of the children to their fathers" (Malachi 4:6).

— **Joshua Hren**, founder of Wiseblood Books, and author of *Contemplative Realism: A Theological-Aesthetical Manifesto*, and *Blue Walls Falling Down: A Novel.*

Published by Scepter Publishers, Inc.
info@scepterpublishers.org
www.scepterpublishers.org
800-322-8773
New York

Cover Image: Artwell from Getty Images
Cover Art: DeLight Design
Text Design and Pagination: Studio Red Design

Paperback ISBN: Print: 978-1-59417-535-0
eBook ISBN: 978-1-59417-536-7

Library of Congress Control Number: 2024944934

Printed in the United States of America

CONTENTS

PROLOGUE

The Upward Arrow is a spiritual book, but not as we may imagine we know that category. I mean it in the best sense: that it places faith in the context of life in the world, which is where it must connect and be connected to, and in the most essential locus of all, which is the family. It is a kind of memoir too, a memoir of that dimension of life that has fallen off the lives of so many nowadays, or shrunk or disappeared, the dimension illuminated for us by what Patrick Kavanagh called "the Flash"—the Other World suddenly manifesting in moments of grace or beauty.

The author claims it is a book "about marriage and the raising of children," a topic he says he addresses as a duty of love. And so he does, and beautifully. It is, then, also a book about the spiritual union of man and woman, and about what flows from this when it occurs in the right way, which he describes as "mutual subjection," one to the other, the other to the one. This mutual subjection arises through reverence for Christ, which is what enables a man and a woman to forget about what they are supposed to be like together and be together as they might if Christ were in the room (which of course he invariably is!).

The central motif of the book is the relationship of the author's parents, Joe and Mary, who started off fighting always and worked their way to not fighting at all. From the Power hearth of his childhood, he strikes out to speak of the modern world and men and women within it, struggling to relate and remain, while struggling also with broken hearts and broken spirits. This struggle will always be contingent, because falling short of one's ideals is the human condition, and, as he says, it is not a bad thing to be always displeased with oneself.

This is a remarkable book. It is a book built on a scaffolding of stories, a book of moments, personal and historical, brought together in what would be called a "narrative"—if the word had not become so misused. It celebrates masculine nobility, a woman who delivers "mom bombs," and the aptitude in children for spontaneous Christian philosophizing. It is not, as one might anticipate, a book of pieties, but a book of deep wisdom, forged on the anvil of vocation, and governed by the motto "It is forbidden to bore."

In this spirit, so to speak, it is also a book of surprises: "Parents," he writes,

> also have the right and the duty to remain happy and hopeful and playful as their children hurtle toward hell. It's your best strategy against Satan, who wishes to sterilize you as an apostle by taking away your peace and joy, turning you into an anti-apostolic nervous wreck. Get on with your own life. God avails of these sufferings to purify parents' hearts, to detach them from their own children, to break and enlarge their hearts so that they may give life and love to other spiritual children in God's plan who need them.

Fr. Colum is the kind of priest people spend their lives looking for and never finding. Here he is, in a little more than a hundred and fifty pages. This book is about as far from boring as it is possible to imagine a book about faith being. It demands your attention, but also earns it, and deserves it when it comes. This book is a thing of beauty in its every word. If you know somebody who has no time for either faith or religion, send them this book with a brief note, culminating along the lines of, "Here is a book about faith that does not preach, does not bore, and may very well change the entire direction of your life." Amen.

John Waters
Author of *Lapsed Agnostic* and *Beyond Consolation: Or How We Became Too Clever for God … and Our Own Good*

Chapter 1
INTRODUCTION

I. AN IMPATIENT PATIENT

Why the title *The Upward Arrow*? I got it from my father. Two years before he died, he called me aside. He was eighty-eight years old, still mobile, but very thin and feeble. The final climb to Calvary was already underway. "I'm not long for this world; the chances are that you're going to preside at my funeral, and you're going to need to know what to say in the homily."

As a priest, I figured I'd get to have the last word at his funeral Mass, but he was way ahead of me right to the end. He proceeded to tell me what to preach. He said:

> When I was a young dentist starting out in Cork, I attended Mass at the Sacred Heart Church on the Western Road. One of the Sacred Heart missionaries told a story about a man named Dr. John. The first thing he said was that this Dr. John character had his clinic for his patients on the third

floor of a five-story building in the city. I perked up at that. OK, I was a dentist, not a doctor, but I had just opened my clinic on the third floor of a five-story building in Cork City. So anyway, this Dr. John fella stuck a bronze plaque on the wall right beside the entrance to the building on the ground floor with the words, "Doctor John, Upstairs" on it, and an arrow pointing upward.

Dr. John wasn't a flashy character. There was nothing out of the ordinary about him. A family man of strong and simple faith, he went about his daily business without much ado. His name never appeared in the newspapers or his face on the television. He was never asked to be president of this or that club or association. And yet, when he died, his funeral Mass was massively attended and traffic came to a halt. Throughout his life he had generated such a current of affection around him that someone plucked that bronze plaque from the entrance to the building and stuck it on his tombstone, so there it was waiting for everyone when the hearse arrived and they carried the coffin to deposit him in the gaping hole in the ground: "Doctor John, Upstairs," with the arrow pointing heavenward.

When I heard that story, I thought to myself, "That's my spirituality! That's how I want to live and die." I'm not saying I've always succeeded because I haven't, but that's how I've tried to live. So, just tell them that, and wrap it up!

It's not easy to preach at your father's funeral Mass, but he made it easy for me. I did as I was told. It went down well.

The night before he died, a couple of months short of his ninetieth birthday, he described himself as the most impatient patient in the hospital. He didn't want to die in the hospital, he wanted to die at home; so he was impatient with the hospital, but he was also impatient to head home, upstairs. My brothers took turns accompanying him throughout the night. When he woke up in the morning he looked around and asked, "Where's Mary?" Mary was his wife of almost sixty years, my mother. As it happened, she wasn't there in that precise moment.

One of his daughters-in-law was there. She answered: "Mary went home to rest. She'll be in shortly."

He raised his right arm and said, "Tell her she's been the love of my life. And, as for you, don't suffer so much about the young fella; I'll take care of him now." With that, he dropped his arm and died.

The young fella he referred to was a grandson, firstborn son of the daughter-in-law sitting beside his bed, who had hanged himself at the age of twenty a year and one month before. She found him dead in the back garden shed after seeing the light on through the kitchen window while preparing breakfast; a mother's worst nightmare.

"Don't suffer so much about the young fella, I'll take care of him now." With his last breath, he left us a luminous legacy of love, faith, and hope, the three theological virtues. God's saving power is well capable of reaching the most apparently hopeless of human situations, suicide not excepted.

Whoever said we'd get this thing they call "closure" here on earth? On the contrary, our Faith teaches that our task doesn't end here. Christ taught that the man who negotiates well with what he is given will be told: "Well done, good and faithful servant; you have been faithful over a little, I will set you over much; enter into the joy of your master" (Mt 25:21). That was the sense of Joe Power's last words: I will be put in charge of many things, among them the salvation of my grandson's soul. It's called the communion of the saints. Between individual judgment and final judgment, there's work to be done in heaven.

It's said that holiness is not about doing great things, it's about doing the little things with great love. There's a beautiful truth in this, but it's not the complete truth. Jesus said that if we are faithful in the little things, we will be faithful in the great ones as well. This implies that every human life is composed of countless little moments, plus a significant quota of big ones also. Every human being must confront the challenge of death; for example, our own death and the death of our loved ones. Those are big challenges, big moments, and there are many others like them: big moments, hard moments, bitter moments, moments that test our littleness and our greatness, our pusillanimity and our magnanimity, our smallness or greatness of soul.

II. A CAVALIER PLAYFULNESS

Spiritual books are often serene and cerebral. Serene is good, and cerebral is good, but in real life there's also the rough-and-tumble, the tragic and the comic, heartbreak and bloodshed. In the Gospels, too; the Gospels are not only, or mainly, serene and cerebral. Shortly after I donned the black cassock as a novice of the religious life in the Servants of the Home of the Mother, people began to approach me for spiritual direction, thinking I was a priest. I was thirty-two years old at the time, but I was only a novice, and I told them so; but people still wanted to tell me their troubles. There's something about the religious habit that still, thank God, awakens people's faith and trust. One couple approached me at a site of Marian apparitions and shared with me that their fifteen-year-old son had recently been killed in a joyriding accident: he and a friend had stolen a car to race against others in another stolen car. There was a crash and both died. Their son was the driver.

Soon afterward I consulted a wise priest: "I'm still the ordinary Joe that I was a few months ago, but people come up to me telling me their personal tragedies looking for answers, and I don't have any!"

He answered, "They're not looking for answers. You must be quiet and listen to them, praying for them and allowing your heart to suffer with them. If the Holy Spirit gives you words to say to them, well and good; if not, that's fine too."

Spiritual counseling must surely factor in the anxiety and even anguish of life, the existential vertigo, and the pull of despair, while at the same time celebrating the triumph of laughter. A cavalier playfulness on the brink of the abyss is characteristic of the true Christian spirit. Our hearts are full of battle scars of all kinds, which are useful experiences that enable us to listen and love and sometimes to speak, or, as in the case of this book, to write.

Nonbelievers question the authority of priests to comment on matters related to marriage and the family: "What gives you the right when you're not married and don't have children?" Firstly, it's not a right, it's a duty of love. Secondly, we were born into a family. Thirdly, we speak to more married people and children than any other category of persons. That provides us with a wealth of experience, and with experience comes authority. Many concrete examples of such conversations will appear in this book.

The subject of this book is holiness in the domestic battle. I am the fifth of nine siblings, all born in ten years; no twins, no girls, all boys. The domestic scenario was a war zone, and my parents were spiritual warriors. I am the son of a happy marriage. Fewer and fewer people can say that. Joe and Mary dated for three years, beginning when she was nineteen and he was twenty. They fought so much they had to give it up. For seven years they went their separate ways, Joe to Yorkshire in northern England and Mary to London, and the future existence of their nine sons hung by a slender thread. In those days, newly graduated Irish dentists preferred not to establish themselves in Ireland. When you're fresh out of university, you tend to make mistakes. Mistakes are bad for business. In this, dentistry is no exception. So, instead, they traveled to England for a few years to avail of the English welfare system to learn their trade while inadvertently wreaking vengeance on Saxon molars for eight hundred years of occupation. (Just kidding, sorry.) Having perfected their craft, Joe and Mary met again back in Ireland after seven years and were married six months later. In almost sixty years of marriage, their sons never saw them fight, but, boy, did they know how to fight! Just not with each other—only with their sons, and against the world, the devil, and the flesh. When people find out that you are one of nine siblings, all boys, the reaction is usually this: "Nine children! All boys! Your poor mother!"

My eldest brother has conceived a good response to this reaction: "My poor mother? If there had been ten more of us, it might have been an even match." In other words, Mary was a strong woman, well able to deal with her nine sons, with plenty of resources to spare.

A few weeks before she died at the age of ninety-four, when the nurse reacted with the usual amazement at the fact that she was the mother of those nine men who kept coming in to visit her, she replied, "Ah, they were never a bit of bother." That was a fib. She went before her Maker with a fib on her soul. Actually, it wasn't just a fib; it was a whopper. But God likes those whoppers: "Blessed are the merciful, for they shall obtain mercy" (Mt 5:7).

Catholic mothers are famously strong women. Even the secularist, anti-Christian culture often portrays them as formidable, while at the same time propagating the claim that Catholicism oppresses women. Irish Catholic mothers of that time had big personalities. I saw this in my mother and in the mothers of my peers. They had authority in the home. The myth of the oppressed Irish Catholic woman is a lie. We've been deceived. They are a slandered generation. They were good people and good times. One of the greatest blessings of my life has been to belong to a numerous family, a blessing that was not uncommon then and is now increasingly rare. In 1971, when I was six years old, almost half of the Irish population was under twenty-five years old. There were lots of children and lots of young people. It was a good time and place to grow up. The advent of artificial contraception and its focus on money and comfort over love and life has caused us to lose more than we've gained. "You cannot serve God and mammon" (Mt 6:24). My mother, a dentist like my father, stopped working to be a full-time mother. Her dignity, personality, and authority were entirely undiminished by this decision. She was a strong woman.

Mary Power was strong, but she was merciful too. The most moving tribute to my mother that I ever heard came from the lips of a convicted criminal. I'm going to say his name was Jerry Murphy, even though it wasn't. He started off as an infantile delinquent, developed from there to become a juvenile delinquent, and matured into a fully-fledged criminal. He was the scourge of the neighborhood: bullying, burglary, glue-sniffing, violence, anything to do with danger. He had red hair, as did most of the Power brothers, and whenever he was interviewed by the police, he said his name was Power. We knew that because the police told us. He spent his youth in juvenile detention and his early adult life in and out of prison.

One evening I set out on what they call a pub crawl (what a wretched pastime). I entered a random pub on South Main Street in Cork City center. It was a den of thieves. By the time I realized what kind of joint I was in, I had already ordered a drink. "OK," I thought. "Let's finish this fast and get out of here."

Next thing, I saw Jerry Murphy at the other side of the pub. He'd been released from prison. He was looking straight at me. After a few minutes, he stood up and walked across the room and sat down right next to me, turning his face toward mine: "You're a Power, aren't you?"

Perhaps I experienced something like what St. Peter felt when the woman said to him, "Are not you also one of this man's disciples?" (see Jn 8:17). I did some very quick thinking only to realize that it was useless: there was no point in denying it; it was obvious that he knew. So I croaked, "I am." (It was nothing like the "I am" of Jesus when his pursuers said they were seeking Jesus of Nazareth as we see in John 18:6).

With that, his ravaged face suddenly softened into the sweet smile of a little boy—I kid you not: it was a beautiful, striking, unforgettable transformation—and the words came out slowly: "Your Ma never stopped saying 'Hi Jerry' to me on the street."

I answered with a surprised "Oh!" and a nervous smile. He got up and returned to his companions; I finished my pint and left. That was one proud moment among many.

Joe was born in 1928, Mary in 1929. That means they grew up as children in the Catholic Ireland of the 1930s, and as teenagers in the 1940s. They were young adults in the Catholic Ireland of the 1950s and young parents in the 1960s. A calumny has been perpetrated against that generation, which should be rebutted. They were tough people, but they were not hard. They understood truth and justice and sacrifice, but they also understood and lived Christian charity and mercy. The week after my father died a man approached one of my brothers on the street and said, "Are you Joe Power's son?" He proceeded to relate that both his parents were dentists and consultants and were one of the first marriages from Joe Power's dentistry class to split up. He remembered the quietness of his house growing up, because after the marriage breakup there were no callers. His parents' friends, disconcerted by a complicated situation, stopped visiting. All except for one couple: Joe and Mary Power called without fail every week and he remembered as a child the lift it gave him that his parents still had friends.

There it is again, see: "Doctor John, Upstairs." Joe and Mary were ordinary people made extraordinary by God's grace acting in them through the sacraments of matrimony, the Eucharist, and confession. That generation gave us a legacy of wisdom and strength that shouldn't be lost. Their approach to marriage and parenting has provided me with endless fodder as a priest for talks and homilies to married couples over the past couple of decades. This book is about marriage and the raising of children, but it's also a defense of a slandered generation, an homage to a forgotten wisdom, and a prayer for my country and the world. A similar book could be written about my aunts and uncles and the parents of my peers. I know this because I knew them, and saw in them the same wisdom, common sense, and often heroic goodness, which is something that cannot easily be said about more recent generations. They were great people *because* of their Catholicism, not despite it. Their testimony, along with countless other experiences and conversations with married couples and young people as a religious missionary priest, coupled with reflections on biblical episodes and Church teachings on marriage and the family, fill the following pages.

Chapter 2
KING AND QUEEN OF THE CASTLE

I. ONE FLESH AND ONE SPIRIT

If you don't like to think much, you can skip this section. It's about Catholic teachings on marriage.

It is true that Christ has told us that there will be no marriage in heaven: "For in the resurrection they neither marry nor are given in marriage, but are like angels in heaven" (Mt 22:30). Too often this has been clumsily interpreted. I have spoken with a widowed mother of six young children who suffered greatly at the idea that in death her union with her husband had come to an end. This is false. Catholicism does not teach that death is stronger than love. We may safely assume that St. Peter is not distributing divorce papers at the heavenly gates.

Pope St. John Paul II and the *Catechism of the Catholic Church* have interesting things to say about the means and the meaning of marital union. Number 2365 of the *Catechism* quotes the words that St. John Chrysostom encourages young husbands to say to their wives:

> I have taken you in my arms, and I love you, and I prefer you to my life itself. For the present life is nothing, and my most ardent dream is to spend it with you in such a way that we may be assured of not being separated in the life reserved for us.[1]

In his "Letter to a Young Widow," Chrysostom is clearer still:

> For such is the power of love, it embraces, and unites, and fastens together not only those who are present, and near, and visible but also those who are far distant; and neither length of time, nor separation in space, nor anything else of that kind can break up and sunder in pieces the affection of the soul. But if you wish to behold him face to face . . . do your best to manifest a life like his, and then assuredly you shall depart one day to join the same company with him, not to dwell with him for five years as you did here, nor for twenty, or a hundred, nor for a thousand or twice that number

1. John Chrysostom, *Homilies in Ephesians*, 20, 8: pp. 62, 146–147, in *Catechism of the Catholic Church*, 2nd ed. (Washington, DC: Libreria Editrice Vaticana–United States Conference of Catholic Bishops, 2000), no. 2365.

> but for infinite and endless ages. For it is not any physical relation, but a correspondence in the way of living which qualifies for the inheritance of those regions of rest.[2]

It's worth recalling in this context that there will be no Eucharist in heaven either, no confession, no sacraments. What then did Christ mean by saying there will be no marriage in heaven? He meant that the souls of all the saved will be directly married, without mediation, to Christ and in Christ to God. This does not exclude the possibility that souls who have been especially united in this life will adore Christ together in eternity. On the contrary, the Catholic tradition has always taught that the closeness of loved ones is one of the joys of the Beatific Vision. St. John Chrysostom's words express the belief that spousal union achieved in this life will be eternalized in heaven. "What therefore God has joined together, let not man put asunder" (Mt 19:6). That much we know because Christ said so. It makes sense that what God himself has joined together, God himself will not rend asunder. Sundering is Satan's job, not God's.

---

2. John Chrysostom, *Letter to a Young Widow*, trans. W .R. W. Stephens, in *Nicene and Post-Nicene Fathers*, vol. 9, ed. Philip Schaff (Buffalo, NY: Christian Literature Publishing Co., 1887), online ed. at New Advent, ed. Kevin Knight, no. 3, www.newadvent.org/fathers/1904.htm.

All of which invites the question: What should this union look like, to qualify for eternal bliss? In his Apostolic Letter *Mulieris dignitatem*—"On the Dignity of Women"—St. John Paul II confronts the infamous words of St. Paul in his Letter to the Ephesians: "Be subject to one another out of reverence for Christ. Wives, be subject to your husbands, as to the Lord. For the husband is the head of the wife as Christ is the head of the church, his body, and is himself its Savior" (Eph 5:21-23).[3] The pope's analysis reflects an acute awareness that he is navigating a minefield both of modern sensibilities and at the same time of traditional sensibilities. The subject is a difficult and delicate one: the relationship between men and women, between husband and wife. Modern sensibilities want us to move forward, ignoring what happened in the past; traditional sensibilities want us to remain in what happened in the past, ignoring the demands of the present.

The Pope of Love must propose the synthesis of fidelity and continuity that is characteristic of the living tradition. He treads very carefully

3. See John Paul II, Apostolic Letter *Mulieris Dignitatem* (August 15, 1988), nos. 23-27, www.vatican.va/content/john-paul-ii/en/apost_letters/1988/documents/hf_jp-ii_apl_19880815_mulieris-dignitatem.html.

indeed, arguing that St. Paul wished to introduce a perennially transformative novelty into the husband-and-wife dynamic: "The author knows that this way of speaking, so profoundly rooted in the customs and religious tradition of the time, is to be understood and carried out in a new way: as a 'mutual subjection out of reverence for Christ' (cf. Eph 5:21)."[4] The term "mutual subjection" should be noted. It has been overlooked by many for many centuries. Pope John Paul II indicates that the conventional understanding that the woman be subjected to the man is being substituted by St. Paul from within by a new idea of a subjection that is not one-sided but mutual. After all, St. Paul specifically says, be subject "to one another," before proceeding to instruct wives to "be subject to your husbands."

Pope John Paul II recognizes that the equilibrium proposed here by St. Paul has not yet been achieved and must be negotiated by each generation:

> However, the awareness that in marriage there is mutual "subjection of the spouses out of reverence for Christ," and not just that of the wife to the husband, must gradually establish itself in hearts, consciences, behavior and customs. This is a call which from that time onwards, does not cease to

4. John Paul II, no. 24.

> challenge succeeding generations; it is a call which people have to accept ever anew.[5]

The Holy Father goes so far as to compare this challenge to the process toward the abolition of slavery, a process that took centuries to complete:

> St. Paul not only wrote: "In Christ Jesus . . . there is no more man or woman," but also wrote: "There is no more slave or freeman." Yet how many generations were needed for such a principle to be realized in the history of humanity through the abolition of slavery![6]

Finally, Pope St. John Paul II repeats the term "mutual subjection" with which he began:

> All the reasons in favor of the "subjection" of woman to man in marriage must be understood in the sense of a "mutual subjection" of both "out of reverence for Christ." The measure of true spousal love finds its deepest source in Christ, who is the Bridegroom of the Church, his Bride.[7]

Prudently, the Holy Father doesn't unpack what "mutual subjection" might mean. Imprudently, I dare to propose an example that might shed light on the matter. Yes, I know, "Fools rush in where angels fear

5. John Paul II, no. 24.
6. John Paul II, no. 24.
7. John Paul II, no. 24.

to tread." If a man as wise as John Paul II preferred to leave the matter open, who am I to propose an answer? And yet the pope himself calls us to respond to this very challenge. Let's not rush to premature inconclusions. Let's hear the proposal, and then see what you think.

II. TESTIMONY OF AN EX-PROTESTANT

One woman told me that her conversion from Protestantism to Catholicism transformed her marriage. Beforehand, having grown up in the 1960s, her mentality was combative, to ensure that she had an equal say in the marriage, in everything. She transmitted that combative mentality to their three daughters. When she converted to the Catholic faith, and read the Scriptures and Church teachings on marriage and the family and the relationship between husband and wife, she came to the decision that, having had her say on whatever matter, she would leave the final decision to her husband, assuring him of her unconditional support, no matter what he decided, and taught her daughters to do the same. A matter of months into this new dynamic, she observed that her husband, no longer fearing her as a rival, had begun to approach her with greater peace and openness and a listening heart, so that she ended up having far more influence not only in the running of the family but also in the running of his business affairs. She had truly become his companion and confidante, and the marriage entered a higher level of friendship.

The woman's "subjection" consisted of allowing her husband the last word in the decision-making process, while the "subjection" of the man consisted of consulting his wife in domestic as well as professional matters. In him, there was a listening mind and a listening heart, a respect and receptivity toward the feminine charism. In *Mulieris dignitatem*, Pope John Paul II explores a richness of wisdom unique to the woman, which the man does not have and would be foolish to ignore. In the case of the Holy Family, St. Joseph exercised an authority as husband and father when it came to making major decisions like fleeing to Egypt and later returning to Nazareth, but he would have been a foolish man indeed not to listen to his wife. In spiritual direction, the priest has an important role, but when spouses live in grace and prayer, each is the other's primary spiritual guide in God's plan. By obeying one another, they are obeying God. Spouses are called, therefore, to an obedience that is *religious* in all senses except the canonical one.

Pope John Paul II also affirms, as we have seen, that the call to mutual subjection "does not cease to challenge succeeding generations." The challenge is not just social and generational, it's also personal: each couple must work it out for themselves with the aid of the Holy Spirit. The example of the converted Protestant feminist and the businessman may not be paradigmatic for all wives and all husbands. As a priest, I have encountered cases where the husband, for example, recognizing his limitations in matters of domestic economy, surrendered entire control of the family finances to his wife, and I have encountered cases where the wife, recognizing her limitations in this same area, surrendered entire control of the family finances to her husband. In both scenarios, the results were entirely positive. I have also known cases where one party or the other is unwilling to accept limitations in a given area, and the results are invariably negative.

III. ¡VIVA LA CONTRARREVOLUCIÓN!

One thing is beyond debate: there must be "subjection." There must be martyrial humility. We have a problem here, because for a typical modern woman, the very idea of being subject to a man is terrifying, unthinkable, a scandalous proposition.

For a typical modern man, the same applies. And yet, without obedience, subjection, and submission, there is no hope of harmony in this life or the next. As a religious priest with a perpetual vow of obedience, "as an unconditional offering of my fidelity to the Catholic Church, to its teachings, and to those who in his name direct it, as representatives of the authority that only proceeds from God,"[8] I am qualified to speak on this matter. Obedience is humbling, not humiliating. Satan humiliates, sin humiliates. Christ humbles, Christ elevates: "Whoever exalts himself will be humbled, and whoever humbles himself will be exalted" (Mt 23:12). Traditionally, in the wedding ceremony, husbands vowed to love and cherish their wives, and wives vowed to love, honor, and obey their husbands. Joe and Mary, my parents, married in the year 1960, and most likely made those vows. We might want to consider bringing back that awful word, "obey."

Joe and Mary were witnesses of a time when men knew how to be men and women knew how to support them, a time when women knew how to be women and men knew how to support them. She had his back and he had hers. Our entire family was

8. Rule of the Servants of the Home of the Mother.

watching a rugby match one Saturday evening, Mom and Dad and their nine sons. Ireland was playing England, the old enemy. Now, the rugby season coincides with the winter season, so a warm fire was glowing in the fireplace. With a matter of minutes left before full time, a penalty was given. We were glued to the television screen. As the famous football manager Matt Busby comically put it, referring to soccer, "It's not a matter of life and death; it's much more important than that."

As the fly half began his run to kick the ball toward the posts, my mother had the bright idea to put some coal on the fire, blocking everyone's view of the TV screen. A spontaneous, unanimous roar urged her to get out of the way. My father stood up, turned off the television, and addressed his sons: "Out, all of you, out; don't ever speak like that to your mother." He didn't raise his voice, but it contained an effective fatherly fury. All his sons knew instantly and instinctively that he was entirely in the right. We traipsed out of the room and then ran to a neighbor's house to watch the remaining minutes of the match, while Mom and Dad turned the television back on and watched it in peace and quiet at home.

For Mary, Joe was the king of the castle; for Joe, Mary was the queen of the castle. The children were not little princes, and even less little princesses. They were subjects. There it is again, that other awful word, “subjects”: *subjection*. We will have to return to this word when it comes to discussing the task of subjecting, I mean *raising*, children (the contrary verbs of raising and subjecting are two aspects of the same task). Obviously, their children didn’t always submit. We often rebelled. In the short term, battles were won and lost; in the medium and long term, the battle was well and truly won. We’ll come to that later.

A few months before she died, I asked my mother how they had succeeded in transitioning from a couple who fought so much that they had to separate to a couple who for almost sixty years practically never fought at all, at least not in front of witnesses. I knew she wouldn’t last much longer in this world and I feared that, when she was gone, I would always regret not having asked. So I did, but it wasn’t a great success: “Ah, that’s so many years ago now, I don’t remember.” I suspect it was a pact of obedience. It may not even have been verbalized. It may not even have been conscious. It was just Christian, that’s all, neither more nor less. Christianity understands that there must be a breaking of mind, heart, and will and a bending of the knee. We don’t like that, but it’s when we’re at our best. This business of bending the knee is bigger than we usually realize. For a major part of our history, the act of bending the knee expressed the spirit of the age. Let me explain what I mean.

Three important things happened in the year 1492: the complete re-conquest of Spain from the Muslims, the discovery of the Americas, and the first meeting of Queen Isabel the Catholic with her new confessor, Fray Francisco Jiménez Cisneros. The queen's previous confessor, Fray Hernando de Talavera, had been appointed archbishop of Granada, which was too far away from the queen's court. The queen wanted a confessor with personality as well as spirituality and de Talavera had won her over with precisely this combination. His would be a hard act to follow. When the queen arrived for her first ever confession with him, she knelt on the other side of the grille and was about to begin but then stopped to say, "Father, the court custom is that, when the queen confesses, her confessor kneels too."

Fr. Hernando de Talavera answered, "Your Majesty, out there, I will kneel before you as a subject before his queen; in here, I represent Christ, King of Kings and Lord of Lords, and you do the kneeling. Kindly continue with your confession." Or words to that effect.

The queen understood and thought, "I have found my confessor."

But now, Fray Hernando was gone, and the queen needed a replacement. Cardinal Pedro González de Mendoza recommended a Franciscan friar named Francisco Jiménez Cisneros, who requires a brief introduction.[9] In his earlier days, Fray Francisco was a clerical careerist, a young man on the make. He knew he was savvy and he had what it took. It was just a matter of letting others know it too, then he would make it big. Off he went to Rome, not to seek his God but to seek his fortune. Sure enough, he was given a position of influence and excelled, so much so, that when he decided to return to Spain, he was given a papal decree to present to the archbishop of Toledo, recommending him for an important post. Fray Francisco presented himself before the archbishop, who said that he would keep him in mind. This was not good enough for our hungry hustler, and he said as much to the archbishop, who had him sent to jail to cool off in the clothes he got hot in (it's an Irish

9. See José Ignacio Ruiz Rodríguez, "M.N. Humanismo cristiano del renacimiento - Francisco Jiménez de Cisneros 2/7," Apr 12, 2019, YouTube video, 26:01, www.youtube.com/watch?v=d9Sy24ACdKw&t=1471s, and José Manuel Marchal, "M.N. La Reforma - El cardenal Cisneros 1/7," Jan 26, 2018, YouTube video, 25:35, www.youtube.com/watch?v=wE2zPZBS5Mo.

expression; I heard it from my mother when she sent me to bed without supper).

Fray Francisco spent two years in jail. At this point, he was thirty years old. Something profound happened to him in jail. When he was finally released, he renounced his worldly ambitions and became a Franciscan friar, a man of prayer and penance, soon gaining a reputation for holiness and wisdom. Some twenty-five years later, when the friar was fifty-six years old, Cardinal de Mendoza sent for him with the good news that he had a position for him now, only to be told, "I don't want a position; I'm happy where I am." But Cardinal de Mendoza would not take no for an answer. When word reached Fray Francisco that the queen's horsemen were looking for him, he fled. He wanted nothing to do with the world now, much less the world of the court and its palatial intrigues. His distaste for social prestige was the best qualification for the job. The queen's horsemen caught up with him, brought him to the palace, and ushered him into the queen's confessional.

Queen Isabel the Catholic submitted him to a test like the one that had produced such a good result with her previous confessor, and Fray Francisco responded that he hadn't come all this way for such nonsense. He had been brought there against his will and was most likely in a bad mood. Again, the queen realized, "I have found my confessor"—a man of spirituality and personality. Fray Francisco Cisneros did not want the job, but he submitted in obedience to his cardinal, to his queen, and to his God: "Thy will, not mine, be done." Years later, when the queen and cardinal expressed the wish to elevate Fray Francisco to archbishop of Toledo, he first refused, but then obeyed again when they insisted. Eventually, with Rome's blessing, he was raised to the rank of cardinal.

From the moment that the queen and the friar first met in 1492, the two heads of power, one secular and one religious, were also two Catholic hearts that beat as one. Cisneros died in 1517, the same year that Luther began his revolution. By that time, the task of true, unadulterated reform of the Church was already done. Together, Queen Isabel the Catholic and her confessor and counselor, Cardinal Francisco Jiménez Cisneros, two counterrevolutionaries and uncanonizable saints,[10] unified and rebuilt Spain and left a Catholic mark on their world so indelible that it is still present in ours, over five centuries later. Their greatness was rooted in their willingness to

10. Uncanonizable only because their historical circumstances compelled them to make tough decisions that the twenty-first-century sensibility finds controversial.

bend the knee before God and one another. Joe and Mary were not Spanish, but they were Catholic, and therefore they were participants in the spirit of kneeling greatness captured in that moment in the queen's confessional. They bent their knees before me on the day of my ordination to receive my first blessing as a priest. They were seventy-five and seventy-four years old at the time, while I was thirty-eight. The shock of that moment is still fresh in my soul. It helped me to understand the confusion of St. John the Baptist when Christ asked to be baptized (see Mt 3:14), or of St. Peter when Christ knelt before him to wash his feet (see Jn 13:8). I was ordained on the twentieth of December 2003, right before Christmas, and spent the first days and weeks of my priesthood looking down in astonishment at God, in the Baby of Bethlehem and in the Eucharist on the altar. One's instinct is to look upward in search of God, and yet Christianity also has us looking downward to find him. It's a bewilderment that has never left me and I pray that it never will.

Abbot Christopher Zielinski remarked once in a conversation with my community, at which I had the good fortune to be present, that if a priest were to sneeze clumsily during the Mass, he could send God himself in the consecrated Host flying off the altar to fall on the ground. He said that God has made himself that small in the Eucharist precisely to stir in the priest's heart and hands a delicacy and carefulness to ensure that nothing like that happens, and that when we emerge from Eucharistic Adoration, that delicacy and carefulness will overflow into our treatment of others. If you are harsh and rough in your interaction with your brothers, chances are that your interaction with the Lord has also been harsh and rough; indeed, the evidence indicates that you have not interacted with him at all.

Christ's trajectory towards his Eucharistic Presence was downward, and ours must be downward also to meet him there. These ideas are not revolutionary, they're counterrevolutionary: *¡Viva la contrarrevolución!* We are born revolutionized, with the mark of Cain on our foreheads; we don't need revolution, we need counterrevolution. "Jesus declared, 'I thank thee, Father, Lord of heaven and earth, that thou hast hidden these things from the wise and understanding and revealed them to babes; yea, Father, for such was thy gracious will'" (Mt 11:25-26). Obedience punctures pomposity and produces unity. For healing and harmony to happen, there must be a downward trajectory into humility and obedience. Let's look now at a humorous biblical precedent.

Chapter 3

THE DOWNWARD TRAJECTORY

I. NAAMAN THE SYRIAN

In the very first sentence of the biblical narrative (see 2 Kgs 5) we are told that Naaman was the important and respected commander of the Syrian army, a great war veteran and victor on behalf of God, king, and country. The second thing we are told is that he was a leper: "He was a mighty man of valor, but he was a leper" (2 Kgs 5:1). The juxtaposition of power and prestige on the one hand with deadly disease on the other is a deliberate pedagogical strategy by the sacred author and the Divine Author. The following passage is peppered with such pedagogical touches. The key moments throughout Naaman's quest for healing are protagonized by "the little people."

For example, an Israelite maid of Naaman's wife suggests that he visit the prophet Elijah, who has special healing powers. Off goes Naaman in search of the prophet with an entourage befitting his social status and mules laden with gold, silver, and precious garments. The pomp and paraphernalia provoke a diplomatic incident when the king of Israel suspects a strategic provocation of war on the part of the king of Syria, but the prophet Elijah intervenes with an offer to settle the question. Eventually, Naaman arrives with his carriage and horses at the door of the prophet's house. Elijah does not come to the door to greet him. Instead, he sends a messenger with instructions for Naaman to wash himself seven times in the River Jordan. Naaman reads this as a snub and climbs up on his high horse, ready to leave in a huff—"Behold, I thought that he would surely come out to me, and stand, and call on the name of the Lord his God, and wave his hand over the place, and cure the leper" (2 Kgs 5:11)—then declares the superiority of the rivers of his own nation to the rivers of the nation of Israel. (This is important. Naaman was required to relativize his patriotism, which is not an easy thing to do; it's a theme we'll have to return to.) Then he turned and made to leave.

Despite his petulance and self-importance, Naaman is loved by his servants, usually a sign of a good man. They were not afraid to reason with him, even addressing him as father:

> But his servants came near and said to him, "My father, if the prophet had commanded you to do some great thing, would you not have done it? How much rather, then, when he says to you, 'Wash, and be clean'?" (2 Kgs 5:13)

This is the third time that God spoke to Naaman through his inferiors: first, through his wife's maidservant, then through the prophet's messenger, and now through his own servants. The words that follow are loaded with significance: Naaman "went down" into the river. Naaman also "went down" into humility. His entire experience with leprosy consisted of "going down" into humility, to the point of allowing himself to be directed, and saved, through his social inferiors.

The journey to healing and harmony is downward. Naaman submitted. The word "seven" represents totality, total immersion, and "according to the word of the man of God" expresses submission and obedience, the result of which is cleanness, purity: "So he went down and dipped himself seven times in the Jordan, according to the word of the man of

God; and his flesh was restored like the flesh of a little child, and he was clean" (2 Kgs 5:14). Naaman attempts to thank Elijah with material gifts, and the prophet refuses. (Prophets prefer poverty; another subject we'll return to.) As mentioned earlier, Christ's trajectory toward his Eucharistic Presence was downward, and ours must be downward also to meet him there. Indeed, Christ's trajectory is similar to Naaman's. Naaman immersed himself seven times in the Jordan, the river in which Christ was later baptized. Christ is Savior and Naaman is sinner, but Christ's salvation involves a sevenfold immersion in the mystery of sin. His baptism in the Jordan points to his baptism on Calvary: "I have a baptism to be baptized with; and how I am constrained until it is accomplished!" (Lk 12:50). Like Naaman, Christ entered this mystery of sin and salvation, and we, like Christ, must enter it too. There are seven main scenes in the Passion of Christ: supper with the apostles, Gethsemane, judgment by Caiaphas, judgment by Pilate, judgment by Herod, the Way of Sorrows, and the Crucifixion. Effectively, Christ's passion is a bloodbath; baptism is a bloodbath. Contrary to Pilate, we say, "I am *not* innocent of this man's blood; this man's blood makes me innocent" (see Mt 27:24), and we immerse ourselves in it. Naaman emerged from the Jordan with the flesh of a child; likewise, when we immerse ourselves with Christ in his mystery, we emerge with the heart of a child.

Confession is also a bloodbath. Dan and I first met in the confessional, and subsequently became good friends. I call him Naaman, after Naaman the Syrian; Dan the Naaman, although his real name is neither Dan nor Naaman. He entered the confessional, confessed his sins, and I gave him absolution. Before he left, I asked him why he was so agitated. I couldn't see him through the confession grille, but it was obvious from his voice that he was agitated. He said there was a line outside and it would take too long, but he was grateful for the expression of interest in his well-being. We arranged to meet. When I saw him, I had to work hard to conceal my surprise; even shock wouldn't be too strong a word. He was wearing a t-shirt and shorts reaching the knees. His face and body, from the scalp of his head to his flip-flop-clad feet, were covered in open sores oozing blood. It wasn't leprosy, like Naaman the Syrian, but it wasn't mere eczema either; it was something much more serious than eczema.

Now I understood why he was so agitated. He smoked constantly and nervously as he explained to me his predicament. The skin disease irritated him constantly, day and night. An ex-military man, he couldn't get a job. He couldn't study. He couldn't sleep more than an hour or two every night when the exhaustion finally became more overwhelming than the itching and his mind and body were able to switch off for a while, until his consciousness became aware of another itch that demanded relief and he was awakened once again to the constant nightmare of irritation. He had tried all kinds of creams and other remedies but nothing worked. The situation was affecting his relationship with his wife, a no-nonsense Russian who was running out of patience. The marriage was already at a breaking point, and his illness was making matters worse.

We strolled along a pathway beside a lake as we talked. I asked him many questions, hoping forlornly to find a solution, to no avail. It seemed like one of those cases where you just listen and pray and allow your heart to suffer, with nothing to offer other than words of compassion and faith in the suffering Christ. We walked and talked several times afterward, and I always came away feeling an immense sorrow for this man and a deep preoccupation for his marriage and future.

At the end of the spring semester, we went our separate ways and I didn't see Naaman again until the following September. This time I didn't have to hide my surprise because it was joyful. His face was red again but this time it wasn't from bloodstains: his cheeks were rosy. There were no open sores or peeling wounds or flakes of skin. He was smiling from ear to ear. I asked him what in heaven's name had happened. A born narrator, he told me:

> I went to see the doctor. The first thing he said to me when I walked in the door was, "Haven't I seen you before, maybe a few years ago?"
>
> "Yes, Doc."
>
> "Did I tell you to give up cigarettes?"
>
> "Yes, Doc."
>
> "Have you given up cigarettes?"
>
> "No, Doc."
>
> "Did I tell you to spend half an hour three times a week in a tanning machine?"
>
> "Yes, Doc."
>
> "Did you do any of it?"
>
> "No, Doc."
>
> "Then tell me, what guarantees do I have that you're going to take me seriously? Why the heck should I take you seriously? Why should I waste any more of my valuable time on you when I could be helping someone else?"

By way of an answer, my friend Naaman shrugged his shoulders and opened wide his arms, saying,

"Look at me, Doc." The logic of those four words was: "I'm in a state of total and urgent need; you're my only hope." And then, this time, like Naaman the Syrian, he finally did what he was told.

Dan's doctor had told him what he needed to do. Dan's wife knew what the doctor had advised, and repeated that advice to him many times as well. So his doctor knew, his wife knew, but he decided that he knew better. Why? Because he didn't want to quit smoking and didn't like the idea of spending half an hour three times a week in a tanning machine. In his self-certainty, Dan had so utterly dismissed his doctor's advice, and his wife's, that he hadn't even mentioned it to me in our conversations. His story is a perfect parable for husband-wife relations and for God-to-man relations (perhaps also for United States-Russia relations). We must present ourselves with our leprosies before the Divine Physician who never says, "Why should I waste my time?"

"And behold, a leper came to him and knelt before him, saying, 'Lord, if you will, you can make me clean.' And he stretched out his hand and touched him, saying, 'I will; be clean.' And immediately his leprosy was cleansed" (Mt 8:2-3). Observe too that the man "knelt before him." When we present ourselves before Christ with our arms open and say, "Look at me, Lord," we are irresistible to him. Strangely, like Naaman the Syrian, we find it hard to do.

The story of Naaman the Syrian is an opportune gateway to enter union with God and union with neighbor. There must be humility, there must be openness to correction and orientation, there must be immersion. "*Look at me, Doc.*" Bathing yourself seven times in the Jordan is not a tall order. Giving up cigarettes and spending half an hour three times a week in a tanning machine is not the end of the world. Nor is receiving baptism and confession and the Eucharist and having a prayer life. We complicate matters and make things more difficult for ourselves than they really are.

Dan's married life was an easy fix too, by adhering to MARC: Mass, Adoration, Rosary, confession. Tanning your soul before the Eucharist is not a hard thing to do. It's easier than giving up smoking, that's for sure. He wrote to me about fifteen years later, by then the happy father of three girls:

> So, as I approach 50, they say your children keep you young and perhaps that is true, I don't know. But they certainly keep you busy, and they have kept us happy and renewed our investment in our marriage many, many times. We know how dreadful it is of parents to abandon their children by divorce. As a teacher, I daily live with

> the consequences of parents' selfishness, and I cannot look into the eyes of any of my daughters and say to them, "I love you, but not enough to sacrifice myself to the vocation of marriage with its daily demands of dying to self, so I am leaving; good luck."

I have another story about MARC. A young lady once consulted me about two young men who were vying for her affections. I had never met her before in my life and haven't met her since. She was finding it difficult to choose between the two suitors and asked for criteria to discern. With gusto, I replied, "Oh, I have a new boyfriend in mind for you. His name is MARC!" Of course, I was thinking of Mass, Adoration, Rosary, and Confession.

Her eyes and mouth opened wide, no kidding. Eventually, staring at me, she whispered in awe, "One of them is named Marc." She thought I was a mystic. For a few seconds, I knew what it felt like to be Padre Pio of Pietrelcina. Scout's honor, this really happened. God's sense of humor, see; the triumph of laughter.

The main lesson of the Naaman story is that it's not complicated. The spiritual life is simple and we might even use the word "easy." "For my yoke is easy, and my burden is light" (Mt 11:30). It's true: Grace can make the hardest things easy. The hard part is humility. We are extraordinarily stupidly stubborn. I have seen so many married couples, good people who love each other, break up because of stubborn stupidity! In spiritual counseling, one is continually unpleasantly surprised by the frequency of basic mistakes. We allow ourselves to get trapped into negative patterns and lack initiative, and especially the humility, to break out of them. Marriages are broken, hearts are broken, and lives are broken, because we don't like subjection. Which reminds me of another marriage, a silent marriage, that was rescued from the brink by the subjection of a wife who succeeded in getting her husband to speak, and eventually to listen.

II. A SILENT MARRIAGE

In Ireland, everyone knows what a silent marriage is: no divorce, no communication. The husband has his life, the wife has hers. Years go by without a word, or with very few words: "Pass the butter," "There's milk in the fridge," "I'll be back next week." And that's about it, the bare minimum. It's not unique to Ireland. It may not have a title elsewhere like it does in Ireland, but it exists.

I knew of one such marriage in Spain. The husband was a university professor and an atheist, the wife was the owner of a small business and a practicing Catholic, and they had two sons in their early twenties who had abandoned the Faith. The father was a bit of a disciplinarian with the boys when they were children, given to the occasional bout of corporal punishment, especially with one of them, the younger of the two. There was a bit of a "personality clash" between father and son. The woman did her best to advise her husband not to get physical with the boy, to no avail. It came to a head one night when the man went to hit his son and the boy, now fifteen years old and quite a beefy customer, pushed his father hard with both hands against his chest and sent him staggering backward against a wall, shouting at him that if he tried to hit him again, he would hit him back.

Thankfully, the confrontation ended there, but so did all communication. The father stopped talking to his sons, the sons stopped talking to each other and to their father, and husband and wife also ceased communicating. Both husband and son were angry with the woman for intervening and for not intervening, without specifying what she should have done, and the wife didn't know what to say or do. She maintained communication with her sons, which made her husband feel more isolated. She tried also to maintain communication with her husband, but there was a barrier she was unable to break, a gulf she was unable to cross. The years went by and the family settled into a pattern of functional disharmony.

As time passed, the ice thickened and became harder to break. During the week, the woman ran her small business, the man gave classes in the university, and the boys attended classes at another university. At the weekends, the woman participated in the local parish life and the boys hung out with their friends. Meanwhile, the husband drove the one-hour journey to his native village where he had inherited a small patch of land. There, he cultivated fruit trees and vegetables, met up with other men of the village for a few pints in the pub on Saturday evenings, and returned home late on Sundays. Then the Cross broke into their lives.

The man suffered a heart attack and was hospitalized for surgery. His wife visited him in the hospital before and after the surgery. He answered her questions and offers of help with gruff monosyllables: "Yes." "No." The word "no" was more frequent than "yes." That was the turning point. The woman realized that something had to be done. This was no way to live, and no way to die. When her husband returned from the hospital and his health returned to normality, she found the occasion to break the silence: "I want something for my birthday this year."

"Oh. What?"

"A pair of gardening gloves."

"For what? You have no clue about gardening."

"I can pull weeds. The rest I can learn. I'm going with you on Saturday to help you in the garden."

Her birthday arrived. No sign of the gloves. She had to purchase them herself. The following Saturday, he got up early as usual and left alone in his car. She had to follow him in hers. By the time she got there, he had already pulled the weeds. Nonetheless, he did show signs of humanity. "He was surprised to see me," she later wrote to me.

> He showed me the peppers, the zucchinis, the different types of tomato, the onions, potatoes, cherries. On Sunday morning, he let me help a little and I had my first trip ever in a tractor at my fifty-four years of age! When I said I had to change for Mass, his face fell a little and I realized that it's true: he's very alone. It wasn't all roses, the weekend, but I've learned that you're happier, big-time, with your heart open and your arms outstretched like Jesus on the Cross, running the risk of getting hurt, than with your arms folded across your chest protecting your heart out of fear of being hurt. I hope I can keep living that way and teach my sons to do the same. My heart does feel a bit raw and defenseless, but I really don't care.

The ice was broken. A river began to flow. Some months later, she wrote:

> I have lowered the bar of expectation. There is no bar anymore. I just accept what comes, enjoy the little things, and am surprised by the bigger things. A little thing, for example, is when he leaves the house very early but sets the table for me before he goes, with slices of toast on a plate. It melts my heart, I can't help it. A bigger thing, for example, is when he waits for me to have breakfast so that I can go with him in his car. On Sunday, we went looking for wild mushrooms. He wanted to do it alone and I had to ask several times. He went in among the thick bushes and I stayed on the trail. Eventually, I too went in among the bushes and, lo and behold, I found some mushrooms! "What a mushroom hunter you are!" he said to me, "I just passed through there and didn't see any!" That greatly surprised me, it was on another level. If things continue like this, he's going to end up convincing me that he loves me a little. There's no turning back now. I don't want to.

The river became a flood. The boy, by then a young man, confronted his father about the episodes of physical punishment. His father expressed sorrow and shed tears. The son shed tears and forgave. A year previously, such a scene was unimaginable. The family vacationed together in an atmosphere of innocent friendship and laughter: "My husband wept with laughter at things I said, at one point saying, 'What did you take with the toast this morning?' The boys laughed a lot too."

Observe that the husband has not yet converted to the Faith, and neither have the sons, but the marriage was saved. That's important. It's a subject we will return to. The relationship must be saved. A family was reunited, thanks to a pair of gardening gloves. Behind the gardening gloves—a birthday present, remember, that the woman had to purchase for herself—there was a heart that was willing, like Naaman the Syrian, to embark on the downward journey to win back for God and for herself her husband and sons. I've seen that in my family too.

III. THE WAR OF THE ROSARY

Every evening my father would bellow the same battle cry: "*Ar bhúr nglúinibh!*" *Ar bhúr nglúinibh* is Irish Gaelic for "On your knees!" In fairness, it sounds a lot worse than it was. It sounds like an authoritarian imposition, like something out of a military boot camp scene in a Hollywood Vietnam movie. Yes, there was authority in it, but mostly it was said with jovial gusto, that's all. "On your knees!" for the Rosary. The family that prays together stays together.

The Night of the War of the Rosary was a before-and-after moment in our sacred family journey. The eldest was about twenty-one and the youngest eleven. For some time, the atmosphere during the family Rosary had been thick and dark and heavy with teenage resentment. Surly and rebellious would also be appropriate adjectives. Things came to a head that night. One son refused to kneel. (There it is again, see? The refusal to kneel.) He continued reading a book. Old Joe didn't even notice until the very end, and asked, "What do you mean by not kneeling down for the Rosary?"

The typically teenage response was, "What do you mean what do I mean?"

Another son intervened: "Don't speak to your father like that."

Two sons faced off, and Joe intervened: "Let it go, let it go." No blows were thrown, thank God, but it was an ugly scene. There was no point in insisting. The battle was lost, the war would have to be fought on another front.

The following night, at the accustomed time, there was a significant silence. What, no *Ar bhúr nglúinibh*? Did this mean we'd finally won? The evening passed without incident. Joe and Mary retired to bed half an hour earlier than usual, and soon afterward the words could be heard through the dining room ceiling underneath the nuptial bedroom: "The Five Sorrowful Mysteries; first Mystery, the Agony in the Garden . . . ."

St. Augustine speaks of his mother, St. Monica, giving birth to him not once, but twice, once physically and once spiritually: "[W]ith a heart pure in Thy faith, she even more lovingly travailed in birth of my salvation."[11] Augustine hints that the labor pains of spiritual birthing are harder and longer than the physical ones. He got that right. That night, in the very bedroom where they most likely conceived their children, Joe and Mary began a new, long, and hard chapter in the birthing process.

A family Ice Age followed, in which each went their separate ways geographically and ideologically, and one cynical teenager (me) was tempted to think, "So much for 'the family that prays together stays together.' Yeah, right, that came true, didn't it?"

Joe and Mary had to behold their nine sons, raised in an Irish Catholic home, become nine insouciant apostates before their eyes. One after another, all abandoned the practice of the Faith. It was a nationwide phenomenon. The materialistic lifestyle was the main factor in the decline of Irish Catholicism, along with a pastoral failure to evangelize the youth. The scandal of Bishop Eamon

11. Augustine of Hippo, *The Confessions of St. Augustine*, trans. Edward B. Pusey, D.D. (Grand Rapids, MI: Christian Classics Ethereal Library), bk. 1, ch. XI, www.ccel.org/ccel/augustine/confess.html.

Casey's affair with an American divorcée hit the news in 1992, when I was twenty-seven years old. It didn't help matters, that's for sure. But, if truth be told, most of my contemporaries had already abandoned religious practice up to ten years earlier, or more. The scandal gave people an excuse. By the time the scandals relating to homosexuals among the clergy preying upon teenage boys were publicized (in a distorted and disproportionate way, with feverish glee, by the rabidly anti-Catholic media), Sunday Mass attendance had already drastically declined.

Joe and Mary lived all of this with sorrow and dismay, but their faith was in no way weakened. If anything, it became deeper and stronger and purer. The crisis in the Irish Catholic Church coincided with a time of significant turmoil throughout the country. In 1972 Bloody Sunday happened, sparking a reign of terror that lasted a quarter of a century. Joe's response? A twenty-five-year fast from all things sweet. Already a non-drinker and non-smoker, he gave up cakes, biscuits, chocolate, ice cream, anything with sugar in it, and sugar itself, at first praying for a united Ireland, and then simply for peace in Northern Ireland. He lived long enough to see his prayers answered on that score, and other prayers too, as we shall see.

Mary was not a crier. Twice in my life I have seen her shed tears, once when I was nine and once when I was nineteen. At the age of nine, I was causing so much trouble with my siblings one Saturday morning that she threw me out of the house and into the back garden. It was raining, an unrelenting drizzle. I took refuge in the coal shed. I was furious: “How dare she throw me out of the house. It’s my house as much as hers!” Oh, the monstrous hardness of a nine-year-old heart! There was a dirty, cobwebby window in the coal shed. Through it I could see my mother preparing the dinner (the midday meal) at the kitchen window. It looked like she was weeping. I rubbed a patch of the black, dust-stained, and webbed coal shed window to make sure I wasn’t mistaken. It was true: there were tears. A shaft of sorrow pierced that bitter little heart: dear God, I’ve made Mommy cry! I went from a fire-breathing fiend to a meek little lamb in less than a second. When she let me back into the house, I saw shredded onions on the cutting board in front of the kitchen window. The cause of those tears? I’ll never be sure.

With the tears that she shed when I was nineteen, there was no room for error. Joe had had a heart attack at the age of fifty-six. His cholesterol and triglyceride counts were normal, as were all his other numbers.

His son-count, however, was high: nine. He almost died and had to have quadruple bypass heart surgery. Mary and I had a conversation. She confronted me about my lifestyle. It began in the living room and I backed out into the hallway looking for a way to escape as she was speaking: "God gave me your nine souls as your mother to get you back to him and be together forever in heaven, and the way you all are going, I'm not going to be able to do it."

And she wept, a bit like Jesus over Jerusalem. St. Augustine called himself "the child of his mother's tears." In my case, those tears didn't bear fruit until twelve years later. That's a story for another moment, a story of family reconciliation and reunion. Let's look now at how Satan divides families, and how God reunites them.

Chapter 4
SATANIC AND NATHANIC MOMENTS

I. A BIBLICAL MARRIAGE BREAKDOWN

The name of King David's first wife was Michal. She was the younger daughter of Saul. We are told twice that Michal loved David (see 1 Sm 18:20-28). She took David's side against her father, helping David to escape her father's murderous wrath by dropping him from the palace window (see 1 Sm 19:11-12). The second window scene in their relationship presents her despising her husband in her heart because of his antics in front of the ark of the covenant containing the tablets of the Law, the staff of Moses, and a particle of manna (triple prefiguration of the new Law of Love, the Cross of Christ, and the Eucharist). David decided to bring the ark to his own home to receive

God's blessing. He stripped himself half-naked and performed all kinds of pirouettes and sacrifices as humble acts of homage before God's sacred presence as the ark made its way to his residence. Michal was watching from the balcony: "As the ark of the Lord came into the city of David, Michal the daughter of Saul looked out of the window, and saw King David leaping and dancing before the Lord; and she despised him in her heart" (2 Sm 6:16). We'll have to return to that word, "despised."

With bitter irony, Michal reproached her husband: "How the king of Israel honored himself today, uncovering himself today before the eyes of his servants' maids, as one of the vulgar fellows shamelessly uncovers himself!" (2 Sm 6:20).

David responds, sticking to his guns: " I will make myself yet more contemptible than this, and I will be abased in your eyes; but by the maids of whom you have spoken, by them I shall be held in honor" (2 Sm 6:22). The final sentence of the story is short and snappy like the lash of a whip: "And Michal the daughter of Saul had no child to the day of her death" (2 Sm 6:23).

The sentence of sterility upon Michal seems to suggest that a bride's contempt for her husband will negatively affect her motherhood. Wives who de-authorize their husbands in front of their children are soon shocked to discover that their children will no longer obey their father or their mother or their teachers or anyone, and everyone ends up losing. I've seen it more than once. It's painful to behold.

However, another question must also be asked: How did David lose Michal? A husband once admitted to me with heroic humility and honesty that, long before his wife betrayed him with another man, he had abandoned her in favor of his cellphone screen. Behind the obvious betrayal of one spouse, there is often a less obvious betrayal of the other. In the case of David and Michal, we know that David was a polygamist. Michal was his first wife, but by the time she turned against him, he had several others, among them Ahinoam and Abigail, whom he appeared to prefer to Michal because they accompanied him in his travels (see 2 Sm 2:2). Then Maacah, Haggith, Abital, and Eglah are mentioned as mothers of David's children (see 2 Sm 3:2–5), and 2 Samuel 5:13 informs us that "David took more concubines and wives from Jerusalem, after he came from Hebron, and more sons and daughters were born to David."

Polygamy was always problematic. Before Christ explicitly condemned it in the New Testament, it was implicitly condemned throughout the Old Testament. Lamech was the Bible's first polygamist. He was the great-great-great grandson of Cain, who murdered his brother Abel. Lamech was more violent than his forefather. He boasted to his wives about his murders (see Gn 4:23). Not a good start for polygamy, which from the beginning also caused envy and disputes and complications between the women themselves and between their children, as in the case of Sara and Hagar and their sons Isaac and Ishmael (see Gn 16:1–16; 21:8–21). Circumcision looks like a corrective consequence of Abraham's polygamous relationship and sexual sin with Hagar. As one scholar put it: "Abraham went astray in Genesis 16, by sleeping with Hagar. Circumcision might be a symbolic rebuke of the part of the body Abraham used when he messed up God's plan."[12] Abraham's son Isaac had just one wife (see Gn 24:67). Moses had one wife (see Ex 2:21). Monogamy worked well for them. Polygamy was always a bad practice with bad consequences, but when it comes to separating husbands from their wives, pornography is worse than polygamy.

Every priest with some level of pastoral experience is aware of the magnitude of the porn problem. It is reconfiguring society before our eyes and yet it is still to a great degree operating under the radar. It needs

12. John Bergsma, *Bible Basics for Catholics: A New Picture of Salvation History* (Notre Dame, IN: Ave Maria Press, 2012), p. 51.

to be flushed into the open. It would be a betrayal of the truth to avoid mention of it in a book such as this one about marriage and raising children, but it requires a separate treatment all of its own. Here, I will confine myself to just a few passing observations and recommendations.

II. INHERITED WOUNDS

It's not easy for a wife to respect a porn-addicted husband. St. Paul urges wives to "respect" their husbands (Eph 5:33), not to despise them, and husbands to "love [their] wives and never treat them harshly" (Col 3:19), to be gentle with them. When St. Paul speaks of contemptuousness in wives and harshness in husbands, he is referring to distinct, inherited wounds in our fallen human condition. It has been said that men need love in the form of respect and admiration, and women need love in the form of affection and attention. The opposite of respect is contempt, and the opposite of affection is harshness. If this is the case, then the enemy of human happiness will seek to ruin marriages by inducing men to be rough and brutish toward their wives, and women to be critical and contemptuous toward their husbands. These distinct, inherited wounds are sometimes comically represented in our general culture.

Toward the end of the film version of *Oliver Twist*, in a song called "Reviewing the Situation," the villain named Fagan, expertly played by Ron Moody, weighs up the pros and cons of criminal life versus married life. Leaning initially toward the married life, Fagan contemplates the risk of being nagged and bled alive for money by a future wife, and concludes he'd better think it out again:

> Better settle down and get myself a wife.
> And a wife would cook and sew for me,
> And come for me, and go for me,
> And go for me, and nag at me.
> The fingers she would wag at me. The money she would take from me.
> A misery she'd make from me . . . I think I'd better think it out again![13]

A funny Protestant pastor has a talk posted on YouTube, with millions of views, about the difference between men's brains and women's brains.[14] He talks about men having a "nothing box" in their brains

13. Ron Moody, "OLIVER! (1968) Ron Moody – Reviewing the Situation," Nov 24, 2018, YouTube video, 4:55, www.youtube.com/watch?v=tAUfaRQk_rs&ab_channel=Cineman%C3%ADadeAyeryHoy.

14. Mark Gungor, "A Tale of Two Brains," Feb 28, 2011, YouTube video, 13:34, www.youtube.com/watch?v=3XjUFYxSxDk&ab_channel=-Monologgruppen.

which women do not have, and claims that it is a man's favorite place to go. When a man is asked by his wife or others what he is thinking about, he shrugs his shoulders and says, "Nothing." His emotional IQ is low or nonexistent. He feels he has an indisputable right to retire as frequently as he wishes to his nothing box. After all, he is doing "nothing" and harming no one, minding his own business and asking only that others mind their business and leave him alone. He is not that much interested in them and simply requires that they not have much interest in him. This seems to him a fair and reasonable deal, not much to ask.

Another song springs to mind, by Mac Davis:

I never get lonesome,
Cause I treasure my own company.
Oh Lord it's hard to be humble,
When you're perfect in every way . . .

I guess you could say I'm a loner,
A cowboy out lone, tough, and proud.
I could have lots of friends if I wanted,
But then I wouldn't stand out from the crowd.[15]

15. Mac Davis, 1974, "It's Hard to Be Humble" in *Stop and Smell the Roses*.

These are comical versions of an oftentimes tragic reality. Simplicity is a masculine virtue, but the kind of simplicity portrayed and parodied here is a caricature of that virtue, a stereotype, based on a wretched reality, that has been propagated and lampooned. Distortions of masculinity and femininity are now as numerous as letters in the alphabet. The figure of the man/husband/father has been sidelined, despised, discredited, and discarded. Now, it's a lose-lose situation. If the man is strong, he's too strong; if he's not strong, he's an embarrassment. A shrill feminist aggression has been unleashed upon the world. It has infiltrated the Church too, of course, and Catholic families. It would be naive to believe otherwise. "I'm Catholic. Therefore I'm unaffected by feminism." No. It doesn't work that way. It's in the air we breathe. We need to take a step back, entertain some self-doubt, activate faith, and then—only then—return to the fray.

Someone sent me an interesting video clip from a bad movie, in which a youngish wife discovers her youngish husband's extramarital affair. She says to him, "So, she's not younger than me, she's not skinnier than me, and she's not prettier than me; then why couldn't it just be me?" The last part of the sentence is delivered with hurt bewilderment.

Then the man answers, "Because she's softer than you, she's quieter than you, she doesn't yell at me, she doesn't call me an idiot or tell me to shut up all the time; she listens to me, she's nice to me, she doesn't make me feel like the only thing stopping her from being happy . . . is me."

The wife responds, "Get out." And that was the end of that.[16]

The chronically disappointed woman is characterized by a hypercritical negativity, an exhausting joylessness. Negativity is her natural habitat. She's in her element there. She doesn't want to leave it. It's a dynamic I have seen in spiritual direction. A priest I know once said to such a person,

> Listen, I don't mind having the blood sucked out of me so long as it's to give love and life, because that gives me love and life too. It's what Jesus did. But if you're going to do it just so that you can continue to die and make me die too, count me out. Do you understand what I am saying?

Faced with constant criticism, the man will retreat further into his nothing box. The more he retreats, the more critical she becomes, feeding the negative dynamic. The children will learn to

16. *The Little Death*, directed by Josh Lawson (2014; Head Gear Films, Australia, 2015).

follow their mother, despising their father. Once they reach adolescence, both parents have lost their authority. Such is the devil's plan. Even if matters never arrive at such a complete breakdown, married couples and families often settle for a milder version of these negative dynamics, far from God's plan.

On one occasion, I was sitting on a bench chatting with a husband. He leaned forward, rested his elbows on his knees, lowered his head and raised his hands to his face, and said, "Father, I can't get a single positive word out of her." He said it with a defeated spirit. A broken heart is one thing, a broken spirit is another. Christ loved us unto the breaking of his heart. We need to have our hearts broken—but our spirits, never. I remember it vividly. His broken spirit broke my heart. They ended up separating. He really wasn't a bad man. Nor was she a bad woman. On the contrary, she was a good person, he was a good person. Two good people who fell in love and married; what the heck happened?

Somehow, at some point, communication broke down. The Good Book says, "Woe to him who is alone" (Eccl 4:10). Neither men nor women are made for being alone. The woman is made for companionship. It's in the Bible: "It is not good that the man should be alone; I will make him a helper fit for him" (Gn 2:18).

Communication is the lifeblood of friendship. When the man wraps himself in a brutish, selfish solitude, he frustrates himself and frustrates his wife. Porn addiction is the logical, sexual, sterilizing expression of that solitude.

Porn addiction causes erectile dysfunction.[17] Masturbation is the sexual consummation of egoism. It's about making love with oneself. Such a man suffers from emotional and spiritual deafness. He needs to hear Christ's groaning "*Ephphatha*" to pierce his selfish heart, to break him out of the autism and mutism that renders him incapable of listening to God or neighbor: Jesus, "looking up to heaven, . . . sighed and said to him, 'Ephphatha,' that is, 'Be opened.' And his ears were opened, his tongue was released, and he spoke plainly" (Mk 7:34-35). As St. Augustine put it, "Thou calledst, and shoutedst, and burstest my deafness."[18] Thankfully, as Augustine has just expressed, when man refuses to embark upon the downward trajectory, he forces God's hand. God

17. See Brian Y. Park et al., "Is Internet Pornography Causing Sexual Dysfunctions? A Review with Clinical Reports," in *Behavioral Sciences* 2016; 6:17. Published online August 5, 2016, in the National Library of Medicine, www.ncbi.nlm.nih.gov/pmc/articles/PMC5039517/.

18. Augustine of Hippo, *The Confessions of St. Augustine*, bk. 10, ch. XXVII, www.ccel.org/ccel/augustine/confess.html.

must intervene. There are eloquent biblical examples of this too.

III. DIVINE INTERVENTIONS

The downward journey is ultimately upward, in God's plan. In Satan's plan, the upward journey is ultimately downward. God intervenes to impel us downward into humility, and Satan impels us upward into pride and hardness of heart. Satan is the great divider. He knows our weak points, but God knows our weak points too, and he has also a word to say and a part to play in this battle. There are Satanic moments in life, and there are Nathanic moments in life. Satanic moments are often sweet, and they are intended to separate the soul from God. Nathanic moments tend to be rough, and they are intended to reunite the soul with God.

The word Nathanic refers, of course, to that moment when the prophet Nathan was sent by God to confront King David with the horror of the king's sins of adultery with Bathsheba and the murder of her husband, Uriah (see 2 Sm 12). By this time, David had moved on from Michal, accumulating new wives for himself, including the wives of others. Nathan told David that cute little story about a poor man who had a lovely little lamb that he was so fond of, until a rich man who had flocks of many sheep took the poor man's little lamb from him and slaughtered it to prepare a banquet for a guest. In "greatly kindled" anger and righteous wrath, David cried, "As the Lord lives, the man who has done this deserves to die" (2 Sm. 12:5).

"You are the man," the prophet instantly replied before spelling out the frightening details of God's oncoming punishment (2 Sm 12:7).

Just as instantly David answered, "I have sinned against the Lord" (2 Sm 12:13).

By his knowledge of David's hidden sins, Nathan revealed that he was a true prophet sent by God, and David knew it; he couldn't not know it. That was David's Nathanic moment. It's one example among many in the Bible and in life itself. It's a sign of a good book, and a good spiritual book should have its fair share of Nathanic moments too. We all have these experiences in which our own soul is laid bare to us and we find ourselves naked and defenseless before God's honest truth. Life is full of them. It's one of God's ways of speaking to us.

Simon the Pharisee had a Nathanic moment with Jesus in his own home (see Lk 7:36–50). When the woman who was a public sinner burst into his home and proceeded to wash the feet of Jesus with her tears and wipe them with her hair, Simon scorned the woman in his heart, as well as this so-called "prophet" who didn't even realize that he was being touched in public by an impure woman. Jesus, like Nathan, proceeded to tell Simon a little story about two debtors pardoned by their creditor, and asked, "'Now which of them will love him more?' Simon answered, 'The one who was forgiven more'" (Lk 7:42-43). Simon is relaxed now, confident, and disarmed, and precisely in this moment Jesus moves in for the killing of Simon's self-image. Jesus first congratulates Simon for answering his question correctly, but then proceeds to defend the woman and even to propose her as an example—a notorious prostitute as a model for a prestigious Pharisee!—telling Simon everything he had gotten wrong as a host, unfavorably compared to her. He did this to Simon, it's worth insisting, in Simon's own home, in front of his peers. This was Simon's "That man is you" moment. The ball was now well and truly in Simon's side of the court—What now? You've had your answer, you've received the proof you sought, so what will you do?

Jesus revealed to Simon that not only did he know who the woman was, he also knew Simon's most secret inner thoughts. He passed Simon's test with flying colors: yes, this man is a prophet, a man sent from God, he has proved it to me, and perhaps he's more than a prophet (as he proceeded to forgive the woman's sins). In public situations like this, even the spectators experience an uncomfortable nakedness. They don't know what to do with themselves: "Please, earth, open up and swallow me!" They may steal a furtive glance at the victim to see how he or she is taking it, while at the same time striving frantically and futilely to make themselves invisible for fear of being similarly exposed. The person on the receiving end will usually put on a poker face in a wretched attempt to salvage some façade of dignity while hoping desperately for the focus to move rapidly elsewhere.

In fact, such moments should be embraced. They are life-changers, heart-changers, mind-changers; golden opportunities of conversion. The Kairos of Divine Grace irrupts into the soul. Layers of convenient self-deception are stripped away. Our hearts of stone are plucked from our chests and we are truly given a new heart and a new spirit with which to live and love (see Ez 36:26-27). There's a legend about the lie inviting the truth to go for a walk together. They reached a lake and the lie invited the truth to join him for a swim. The lie dived in first and encouraged the truth to follow him, that the water was cool and fresh. The truth dallied a little longer, removing its clothes.

When the truth eventually entered the water, the lie hurried out and clothed itself in the truth's garments, leaving the truth without clothes. And ever since, people tend to welcome the elegantly clad lie while balking uncomfortably before the naked truth. Thus far goes the pagan legend. Christ crucified is the Naked Truth, the Divine Fool, from whom people foolishly "hide their faces" (Is 53:3), when they should do precisely the opposite: "They look on him whom they have pierced" (Zec 12:10).

Did Simon the Pharisee flinch and turn away his gaze, choosing enraged rejection of the prophet by whom he had been publicly humbled, or did he meet his gaze and bravely surrender? St. Luke the Evangelist doesn't spell out for us what happened in Simon's heart behind his poker face. We have only one clue: Who was St. Luke's source for knowing Simon's secret thought process leading up to Christ's *in apropos* story that took his guard down? Did Christ tell someone, who later told St. Luke? That seems highly improbable, perhaps even impossible: it would be a betrayal of a soul's intimacy. Did St. Luke merely deduce it? That seems unlikely too; it would be a dishonest speculation. Or did Simon himself tell him? If Simon gave St. Luke his interior testimony, which seems somewhere between possible and probable, it would indicate that Simon received his Nathanic moment like David did, and converted. In any event, the main purpose of the entire episode is not so much to ask how Simon lived his Nathanic moment as to ask how you are living yours.

IV. LOOK AND LISTEN

A young woman lamented that she almost always left Sunday Mass feeling a little sad, that she wasn't a good Catholic, that she wasn't living up to what God expected of her. Don't we all feel a bit like that? Is it necessarily a bad thing? Should I leave Sunday Mass feeling pleased with myself for being such a good Catholic? St. Thérèse of the Child Jesus wrote, "If you are willing to bear in peace the trial of not being pleased with yourself, you will be offering the Divine Master a home in your heart."[19] This implies that being displeased with ourselves is not such a bad thing. It's a prerequisite for inner union with God. If you're accustomed to a constant dissatisfaction with yourself, congratulations, you're on the right track! But you must bear it with peace, because even as he

19. Thérèse of Lisieux, "Letters of Soeur Thérèse to Her Sister Céline," March 12, 1899, Letter V, in *The Story of a Soul: The Autobiography of St. Thérèse of Lisieux With Additional Writings and Sayings of St. Thérèse*, www.medjugorje.ws/en/articles/therese-lisieux-story-soul/17.

calls you on to greater things, his forgiveness of you is enthusiastic, his patience with you is infinite, his plan for you is perfect.

Permit me to narrate here a Nathanic parable. It's also scatological. To preempt scandal, remember that Jesus asked, "Do you not see that whatever goes into the mouth passes into the stomach, and so passes on?" (Mt 15:17). He wasn't squeamish about the basic corporal functions. During the time this story happened, I was spending a lot of time studying in a library that was used mostly by priests and seminarians. Every morning, I was the first to arrive. I had a typical established routine: leave the computer on the table near a window and my coat over the back of the seat, and make my way to the restroom, before returning to attack the books. There were three urinals and three toilet bowls. Invariably, there were stains on the porcelain. Somehow, some of the library users had reached the age of adulthood without being taught what the little white scrubbing brush in the corner is for. It bothered me to think that the cleaning lady had to see that every morning. What would she think of priests and seminarians?

And so, every morning, I went about my business, quickly cleaned the stains in the three toilets, washed my hands, and returned to my seat near the window.

One morning, as I scrubbed virtuously, there was a loud knocking noise on the locked door behind me. It was more of a banging noise than a knocking. I opened the door, already a bit nervous. It was the receptionist from downstairs. He was gesticulating and expostulating at me in Italian the way that Italians so expertly do. Then he pointed to the floor. There were stains of dog excrement on the floor in the shape of the soles of my sandals. He led me to my seat and then down the stairs, following a trail of smelly stains on the carpet and the tiles all the way down to the entrance of the building. I didn't know Italian but I knew exactly what he was saying. I was mortified.

In prayer, the Lord let me know that in the to and fro of my virtuous daily life, I was putting my foot in it here, there, and everywhere. I knew what he meant too. One usually does. We go about our daily business subconsciously aware of our habitual clumsiness in our dealings with God and neighbor, and every so often the Lord pulls us up, making us conscious instead of subconscious. That's when it's time for seven dips in the Jordan—a good confession. The Lord is infinitely patient and merciful, and insistent in the call to conversion. Penitents often say in the confessional, "I always come with the same sins, Father." Well, it's not about inventing new ones. God always comes with the same thing too: exuberant forgiveness.

Repeated confessions often build up to a transformative before-and-after moment. They have a cumulative effect. The soul's hatred of sin is gradually strengthened and then, suddenly, after a long battle with many failures and endless forgiveness, the breakthrough happens. St. Ignatius of Loyola said, "One energetic act is worth a thousand that are listless."[20] I heard a young man declare that he realized that he would never be truly free unless and until he had it in him to hate a certain sin to the point where he would rather die than commit it. That became his prayer. He begged God insistently for a holy hatred so that at the slightest whisper of that temptation, he would recoil from it in horror, preferring even death. His prayer, previously "listless," suddenly became "energetic." His holy hatred of impurity was joined to a holy love of manly chastity, loyalty, nobility, honesty, wisdom, and inner freedom. Sure enough, his prayer was soon answered, totally answered: the before-and-after moment finally happened, and he has never

20. Ignatius of Loyola, "To the Fathers and Brothers Studying at Coimbra," Rome, May 7, 1547, *Selected Writings of St. Ignatius of Loyola*, with commentary by Joseph N. Tylenda, SJ, p. 22, https://library.georgetown.edu/woodstock/ignatius-letters#index, consulted 26 March 2024.

looked back. He is now a loyal husband and manly father to six children. It's helpful to set our sights on the beauty of our goal.

V. LAPS WITH THE PONY

A priest I know was told mystically by Mother Mary: "My son, do not set your gaze so much on the negative; fix your eyes rather on so many beautiful gifts that my Son is continually presenting to you." That's good advice for priests but also for husbands and for wives.

Once, I was in the company of an elderly couple who were reminiscing about visits to the woman's family farm (inherited by her brother) with their children when they were young parents. In a tone of awe, she said to her husband, "My goodness, Joe, how patient you were with the children leading that pony around that field one after another, lap after lap, hour after hour until they were all satisfied!" I was flabbergasted. The elderly couple I'm referring to were my parents, Joe and Mary. Something in the region of forty years had elapsed between those visits to the farm and that conversation. In those forty years, Joe had committed countless acts of impatience that she could have chosen to dwell upon, and yet, forty years later, Mary was able to express appreciation of his patience with the children with a freshness, amazement, and devotion as if it had occurred a matter of days earlier!

Mary had a nickname for Joe. She called him "my Nathanael." It's Christ's only direct face-to-face compliment in the gospels. On a handful of occasions (perhaps less than a handful because it was fewer than five), he praised people for their faith, and he praised St. John the Baptist, in his absence, for his greatness of spirit. But only once ever does he praise someone, in their presence, for their virtue, and it was the virtue of manly innocence. Of Nathanael, and to Nathanael, he said: "Behold, an Israelite indeed, in whom is no guile" (Jn 1:47); no duplicity, no secret agenda, no porn, no hidden life. He's a simple man with a noble heart, incapable of lying. That's why porn is so damaging: it foments furtiveness, it diminishes masculine nobility.

If male harshness and female contempt are typical diabolical threats to married bliss, then their opposites—male gentleness and female admiration—are their divine antidotes. The antidote to "nothing box" jock insensibility is loyal affection, and the antidote to endless nagging is joyful admiration. The opposite to "despise" is "admire." Mary immensely admired Joe, as Joe did Mary. Mary brought Joe breakfast in bed every morning, Joe took the tea towel in his hands and dried the dishes. Each was number one for the other, and they knew it.

The same woman who told me about the change in her approach to her husband (see chapter 2), also told me that, soon after her marriage, she consulted her father about something in her life that required wise discernment. She enjoyed an excellent relationship with her father from childhood through adolescence to adulthood as a young woman. To her great surprise, however, her father said to her, "What are you asking me for? You have a husband now. Go talk to him about it." Taken aback at first, she quickly realized that her father had given her the wisest possible advice in her new circumstances. The hierarchy is as follows: in first place, God; in second place, in God, my spouse; in third place, in God, the children; and in a distant fourth place, in God, my birth family and in-laws. By "in God," I mean in love and truth and openness to the Holy Spirit and to Mother Mary, Seat of Wisdom.

Joe and Mary bid each other goodbye with a kiss at the beginning of every day as he set off on his bicycle to work, and greeted each other with a kiss when he returned home. Every day they spent fifteen or twenty minutes alone together after lunch and longer in the evening. Every Wednesday evening, they went out together alone to the theater, to meet with married friends, to go for a walk, or some other leisurely activity. Every Sunday there was a family excursion to the farm or the coast. Every July the family spent three weeks at a rented house in Ardmore, County Waterford, on the southeast coast. Their nine sons were not princes. Their role was to be subjects. We talk about "raising" children, which of course makes sense, but maybe we should talk also about "subjecting" them, or at least about teaching them to subject themselves.

Chapter 5

BRINGING UP CHRISTIAN PHILOSOPHERS

I. INFANTS AND THE EXISTENTIAL CRISIS

An atheist mother told me a true story about her five-year-old daughter, Olivia. Olivia was sitting on the floor playing with her toys. Then she picked up a book, one of those big hardcover books with vivid drawings and lots of colors on each page. It was a children's book about dinosaurs. She was engrossed in it for a while.

Then she said to her mother, "Mommy."

"Yes, honey."

"Is there a zoo where we can go and see the dinosaurs?"

"No, Olivia, there's no such thing as a zoo with dinosaurs. There are no dinosaurs."

"What do you mean, there are no dinosaurs? There are pictures of them here in this book."

"Yeah, but they don't exist anymore. They're extinct."

"Extinct, what does that mean?"

Her mother was getting nervous now, as adults tend to do when faced with the very questions they usually flee. "It means they're dead."

"What does dead mean?"

"It means you stop breathing, your heart stops, you die."

"Then what happens?"

"What happens after you die? Nothing. They dig a hole in the ground, they put you in it, then they cover you with earth, because you're dead."

"Us too? Not just the dinosaurs?"

"Yeah, us too, everyone, everything, we all die, sooner or later, just like the dinosaurs."

"Ah, OK." And that was that. Chirpy as a robin, she went on reading her book and playing with her toys.

See? Children are simple and adaptable; they don't need all these myths to keep them happy. Not so fast. Olivia's mother was awakened at about two o'clock that night. She thought she heard the little girl crying in her bedroom. She got out of bed and went to listen at the door. Sure enough, Olivia was awake and crying, sobbing softly into her pillow. Her mother gently opened the door and entered the room without turning on the light. She sat on the edge of the bed and caressed her daughter's face with her hand, asking her what was wrong. The little girl was trying to stop crying, trying to be brave, fighting to get her act together. Eventually, she sat up and blurted out: "I don't want to die, Mommy. I don't want to be put into a hole in the ground. I don't want them to throw earth on top of me." Then she started shaking and threw her arms around her atheistic mother, who had no answers. Worse still, Olivia's grown-up mother, unlike her five-year-old daughter Olivia, had no questions.

The main lesson to be drawn from this episode is that children are not stupid or superficial. In a sermon on marriage and the education of children, St. John Chrysostom tells parents that they should bear in mind that they are "bringing up a Christian philosopher."[21] On a flight from Spain to the US in the year 2001 to lead my first ever summer camp for boys, a wise priest remarked, "If we can just get them to think, the battle is half-won." It struck me as a smart

21. John Chrysostom, https://thoughtsintrusive.word-press.com/2014/06/25/bringing-up-children-according-to-st-john-chrysostomos/, consulted March 25, 2024; the quotations from St John Chrysostom are taken from the book *Goneis kai paidia* [Parents and Children] by Fr. Philotheos Pharos and Fr. Stavros Kophinas, published by Akritas (in Greek).

approach when I first heard it. I figured, "OK, I can try that." It worked. I've used it ever since. Children are truth-seekers by nature. That's not something to squash, it's something to stimulate. It's about stirring in them the detective spirit. They take to it like a duck to water. With adults, it's more difficult. (If you skipped the first section in chapter two because you don't like to think much, now's a good time to go back and take it on). As adults, we renounce the big questions and settle too easily for an unquestioning materialism. It's a recurring theme in the Gospels.

The Lord's requirement that we have a critical, questing, questioning mindset is expressed on multiple occasions. One such occasion occurs in the Gospel of St. Mark. If there were a prize for the most comical passage in Scripture, chapter 8, verses 14-21, of St. Mark's Gospel would be a serious—comical—candidate. It happens soon after one of the miracles of the multiplication of the loaves and fishes. The twelve are with Jesus in the boat, and they realize they've forgotten to bring bread. They had brought just one loaf for thirteen grown men. Jesus tells them to beware of the leaven of the Pharisees and the Herodians. Hearing the word "leaven," an ingredient in the making of bread, the apostles think he is rebuking them for forgetting the bread.

With this, Jesus has had enough: "Why do you discuss the fact that you have no bread? Do you not yet perceive or understand? Are your hearts hardened? Having eyes do you not see, and having ears do you not hear?" There follows a robust question-and-answer exchange in which Jesus shakes them up like a stern schoolmaster with dull students: ". . . do you hear? And do you not remember? When I broke the five loaves for the five thousand, how many baskets full of broken pieces did you take up?"

"Twelve."

"And the seven for the four thousand, how many baskets full of broken pieces did you take up?"

"Seven."

"Do you not yet understand?" (see Mk 8:14–21).

The episode has its funny side and its serious side. The apostles are still thinking of their bellies more than their souls: "Truly, truly, I say to you, you seek me, not because you saw signs, but because you ate your fill of the loaves" (Jn 6:26). Still fixated on the sign, they are failing to make that leap from the signifier to the signified, from the material to the spiritual. They are guilty of the sin of materialism, manifested also in Capernaum, where many of his followers stuck to a materialistic interpretation of the Eucharist and abandoned Christ. In the exchange in the boat, and on many other occasions, Christ strives vigorously to stir in them a more meditative mind and heart.

A brother priest once said to me that he had observed two common denominators in families that had successfully transmitted the Faith from generation to generation, from parents to children: poverty and a critical mindset. It makes sense. The more tied we are to the material, the clumsier we are when it comes to thought and prayer; the freer we are from the material, the freer we are for the flight of the soul to God. That's why prophets prefer poverty, as we saw earlier. Poverty and a critical mentality go together. God's word aims not to entertain but to hit and to humble. He wants them to be poor, and he wants them to be deeper thinkers. That includes children, as the following historical example demonstrates.[22]

Ven. Louise of France was born in 1737 and died fifty years later in 1787. Louise was a lively and likeable little princess, and obnoxious at times. A nun named Sr. Françoise Pâris de Soulanges was appointed to tutor the princess, and to correct her haughty temperament. Sr. Françoise understood that the

22. See Thérèse Louis Latour, *Princesses, Ladies, and Salonnières of the Reign of Louis XV*, trans. Ivy E. Clegg (London: Kegan Paul, Trench, Trubner & Co., 1927), p. 317ff, https://archive.org/details/in.ernet.dli.2015.66391/page/n317/mode/2up?q=Soulanges.

education of children is not always about affirming them; sometimes it's about denying them. It's not always about saying yes, it's also about saying no. It's not only about building them up, it's also about knocking them down from their pedestal, perch, or high horse. And she went about her task with a ruthless mercy, charity, and wisdom: to build this child up, I must knock her down.

The princess enjoyed seeing the servants' curtsy when she entered the room, so she spent a lot of time exiting and entering rooms to provoke this act of homage to her royal identity, until one day one maidservant failed to bow and bend the knee, either because she didn't notice the princess enter or because she was fed up with this royal pantomime. Princess Louise berated her: "How dare you not curtsy when I enter the room! Am I not the daughter of your king?"

The servant girl, prepped by the wise nun, Sr. Françoise, replied, "Yes, Madame, and I, am I not the daughter of your God?"

The response shocked the princess. It wasn't a "mom bomb," it was a "maid bomb." We can imagine her internal monologue:

> Yes, it's true, she is a daughter of God, and God is greater than the king, but so am I a daughter of God, and I am also daughter of the king, so that makes me more important, and she must curtsy before me, and I must curtsy before God, because God, God . . . How should I treat her as a daughter of God? What does it really mean to be daughter of the king? What does it really mean to be a daughter of God?

Not long afterward, members of Louise's family began to die one after another, reaching a total of seven deaths. Louise's inner process of reflection, awakened by the maid bomb, opened her eyes to the banality of court life, and so she renounced her royal inheritance and entered a Carmelite convent. There, she became an exemplary religious, embracing poverty, chastity, and obedience side-by-side with the other sisters of lower social rank, with a perfection that won her the position of prioress of the community. She acquired a reputation for wisdom that drew members of the nobility to consult her regarding affairs of the court. Her final words before death at the age of fifty were, "To paradise, haste, haste, full speed." From princess to lioness; however, this journey is not exclusive to princesses or nuns, as we will see.

II. LETTERS FROM THE THREE WISE MEN

Princess Louise gave up her royal inheritance in favor of her divine inheritance. The Lord, through a smart nun, knocked Louise down to build her up. A Spanish father I know artfully did something similar. He was so disgusted one year by his children's behavior on the morning of the sixth of January, Feast of the Epiphany, that he begged the three wise men to bring no gifts the following year. (In Spain, Santa Claus has not yet supplanted the three wise men). What was the point? The gifts, intended to produce joy and harmony, produced only bickering and division.

Instead, to everyone's surprise, on that emotional morning the doorway to the dining room, where the gifts were usually deposited, was covered with a white sheet with a blue envelope stuck to the middle of it. Inside the envelope was a letter. The three wise men had written a letter to the children, requiring that it be read aloud by the eldest child before they all opened their Christmas presents. The letter began, "Dear María, Ana, José, Mónica, Gracia, Pedro, Rafael, Clara, and Francisco," and ended with, "Signed: Melchior, Gaspar, and Balthasar."

The letter proceeded with some words of wisdom for each child: some of correction and some of encouragement. Here's a wee taste:

> Dear Gracia, how grown up you are now! The life of the party; beautiful, agile, studious, sporty. Jesus is about to make you understand so many new things that will fill you with enthusiasm. You'll see very soon that you don't need so much of all that which doesn't really fill you. Jesus is about to put you inside his heart, as he's done with Mom and Dad and so many others. What a rest it is when that happens, you'll see.
>
> Pedro Miguel and José Gabriel, each in your own way, you make the Child Jesus laugh. Teach that joyfulness to your little brother Rafael. Jesus says that he gave him to you and that you leave him aside more and more and that makes him sad. Help him to control himself and you will have a great ally in him until the end of your lives.

The man himself was astonished at his children's reaction. He wrote to me:

> That Epiphany morning was the most peaceful ever lived in this numerous family. They shared their toys. They talked with each other about the letter and felt loved by their royal majesties and loved each other. My wife and I couldn't get over it. Even as the children grew up, they continued to receive that annual letter with the same emotion as the first year. Each letter marks the occasions of the preceding year: Communions and confirmations, congratulating them on their achievements, calling them to battle, comforting them in their sufferings, reminding them that all glory must go to the Babe of Bethlehem. Even now that the older ones have left home, they still call us on that morning to ask for a photo of the letter from the three wise men which

> they treasure in their hearts as a reminder that they are children of God and brothers and sisters of Christ and one another, co-heirs of the kingdom of heaven. Thus, the consumerist fever has been transformed into an aid in the transmission of the Faith and a proof of the freedom and wonder of not having to run with the pack.

Sometimes, the negative energy that parents spend chastising and correcting can be better spent creating and encouraging. As a synthesis of knocking down and building up, subjecting and raising, the annual letters of the three wise men are miniature masterpieces, combining truth and love, touching the heart, strengthening the will, and stirring the intelligence.

III. A CRITICAL MINDSET

Stirring children's critical intelligence is an urgent necessity. Christ calls us to sagacity in this regard, lamenting that "the sons of this world are wiser in their own generation than the sons of light" (Lk 16:8), and urging us to be "as wise as serpents and innocent as doves" (Mt 10:16). We twenty-first-century Catholics are surrounded by lies on all sides. A massive, multifaceted propaganda machine bombards us daily. As far back as the 1920s, long before Joseph Goebbels appeared on the scene as the

Nazi minister for propaganda, a man named Edward Bernays, nephew of Sigmund Freud, wrote,

> The conscious and intelligent manipulation of the organized habits and opinions of the masses is an important element in democratic society. Those who manipulate this unseen mechanism of society constitute an invisible government which is the true ruling power of our country.[23]

Bernays was contracted by Lucky Strike cigarette manufacturers to expand the tobacco industry by persuading women to smoke cigarettes. He did so by calling them "Torches of Freedom," and by stationing young women participating in Holy Week processions while smoking cigarettes at strategic points where photographers could get good pictures of them. His campaign was so successful that the U.S. government contracted him to stir public opinion in favor of internal interference and regime change in the government of Guatemala, in order to retain control of that country's natural resources. (Really. Look up Operation PBSUCCESS.)[24] Children and young people should be informed of such events,

23. Edward Bernays, *Propaganda* (New York: Horace Liveright, 1928), p. 9.

24. For example, see The George Washington University, The National Security Archive, "CIA and Assassinations: The Guatemala 1954 Documents," https://nsarchive2.gwu.edu/NSAEBB/NSAEBB4/.

even in the history of their own country. They must be taught not to settle for what they are told by the media or even by their classroom textbooks. They must be encouraged to seek beyond the slogans and the taboos and the dominant narrative. We saw earlier that Naaman was required to relativize his patriotism, not an easy thing to do: "'Are not Abana and Pharpar, the rivers of Damascus, better than all the waters of Israel? Could I not wash in them and be clean?' So he turned and went away in a rage" (2 Kgs 5:12). As I said, it's a theme we would have to return to.

Christ did not say, "woe to the British," or "woe to the Americans," or "woe to the Russians." He said, "woe to you that are rich" (Lk 6:24), and elsewhere, "the rulers of the Gentiles lord it over them, and their great men exercise authority over them" (Mt 20:25). The Gospels recount Christ's difficulties in the task of converting his people from tribalism to universalism, universalism being another word for Catholicism. When two-thirds of the Irish population voted in favor of abortion and homosexual marriage (as if that were even possible), I didn't know how to process it, and the Lord spoke to my heart: "If I wept for Jerusalem, who are you to expect not to weep for your country too?" Our patriotism, like Christ's, must be critical. To have a critical mindset toward one's own country is not easy, and yet, as Catholics we're called to do just that. Unfortunately, sometimes a man will betray his wife more readily than his nation.

The chronicler Callisthenes was a man who refused to betray his conscience by bowing before his emperor. He was a relative of Aristotle and a member of the inner circle of Alexander the Great. A respected historian, he accompanied the great emperor on his military expeditions and competently recorded his heroic deeds for posterity. But when Alexander the Great decided to declare himself a god and demanded the corresponding worship, that all kneel before him, Callisthenes dissented. He reasoned to Alexander that he was deserving of all the recognition of human greatness, and that he had no difficulty in rendering to him such homage, but that in good conscience he could not offer him worship as a divine being. Alexander the Great kept his counsel and bided his time. Callisthenes was eventually arrested, imprisoned, and then executed, some sources say by crucifixion, for refusing to kneel before the emperor. If he suffered the fate of Christ for refusing to bend the knee before anyone but God, I wonder, will we meet Callisthenes in heaven?

Callisthenes refused to kneel before Alexander the Great, and died for it; Queen Isabel the Catholic knelt gladly before Padre Francisco Jiménez Cisneros, and confessed her sins. Those are the options. You either kneel before the state, or you kneel before God. Citizens must at least be taught about this choice, without imposing on them either option. The state will not perform this act of education. It's up to parents. Chesterton famously said that, when he abandoned Protestantism and entered the Catholic Church, he took off his hat, not his head. Taking off your hat is a gesture of respect; taking off your head is an act of suicidal self-mutilation. Our heads are not just for separating our ears. God wants us to be critical thinkers. To ready them for the hormonal assault of adolescence, children's intellects should already be highly developed. Critical questioning is a virtue in every field of intellectual investigation, be it the sciences, history, or philosophy. It's also a virtue in the field of the Faith, Church teachings, and Church actions. There's no such thing as an indiscreet question; only indiscreet answers.

IV. ALL OR NOTHING

Here's an example of an "indiscreet" question that provoked a very discreet answer. A bank manager attended a religious ceremony in which several young women, one of whom was related to the bank manager, received the religious habit. On his way to the party afterward, the bank manager remarked, "How on earth can these young women give up everything for nothing?" One of the young women happened to be nearby and overheard him. She said to him, "You are mistaken, sir. We haven't given up everything for nothing; we have given up nothing for everything." Christian poverty is about giving up nothing to gain everything.

The closest Christ comes to saying, "All or nothing," is recounted in the Gospel of St. Luke, when he compares the kingdom of heaven to a man who sets out to build a tower without sufficient resources to finish it and is mocked by observers, or a king who foolishly enters battle against another king whose troops outnumber him two to one. He concludes: "So therefore, whoever of you does not renounce all that he has cannot be my disciple" (Lk 14:33). It took me a long time, I must admit, to figure out the connection between entering battle and building a tower and the call to absolute poverty, but then suddenly the message became clear: if you don't mean to complete the construction, if you don't mean to win the battle, don't even start. And the key to completing the construction, to winning the battle, is radical, total poverty; every disciple of Christ, celibate or married, must renounce all his possessions. I have seen this instruction brought to life.

God put in my path a young family, two parents and three small children, who had emigrated from South to North America, where they established a successful business. Then the crash of 2007-2008 happened and the business went bust. They now had nothing to live on but their savings. America is not a good place to live on your savings. The months went by, opportunities didn't arise, and the coffers dwindled rapidly. The husband already had a depressive tendency; the situation made matters worse. Eventually, he said to his wife: "I took out a life insurance policy when things were going well. If anything were to happen to me, you and the children will get a million dollars. It's the only way left that I can be of use to you." The implication was clear: suicide and fraud.

His wife answered: "Don't be stupid. I don't care if the five of us have to live under a bridge so long as we don't lose the Faith."

What a sentence! What a woman! She had a squeaky voice. I wasn't expecting that from someone with a squeaky voice. Comically, she had the voice of a mouse and the heart of a lion. Better to have the voice of a mouse and the heart of a lion than to have the voice of a lion and the heart of a mouse. Surely this is what Christ meant when he said, "So therefore, whoever of you does not renounce all that he has cannot be my disciple" (Lk 14:33).

Thankfully, this woman and her husband obtained employment soon after undergoing this tough trial which she passed with such heroic faith. Her love for God was stronger than her fear of insecurity and even of death. Observe that she was not a nun; she was a wife and mother of three small children.

Joe and Mary understood poverty. We were the last children in the neighborhood to discover that the Incredible Hulk was green: everyone else had a color television when ours was black and white. To ferry his wife and numerous offspring to and fro between Mass and other places, my father purchased a nine-seater bright orange Volkswagen minibus. He must have gotten a discount for the gaudy color, which was also the color of most of his children's heads. They call us redheads but it's more orange than red. In Ireland, the Irish Travellers—an itinerant people, similar to the Romani or "Gypsies"—are often redheads. Teenagers like to pass unnoticed, fearing the mockery of their peers. As a small troop of bright orange heads in a bright orange minibus, passing unnoticed wasn't possible. Old Joe didn't care. It was a good deal. One of his nine sons asked, "Daddy, how much did the car cost?"

The answer was, “Oh, a lot of money!”

One of my brothers was out one night at a pub in Cork City center with his buddies. There were two new faces in the group, friends of a friend. They were from a rough part of town, colloquially referred to as “the untamed world,” a name taken from a popular wildlife series of that time. During the conversation, someone mentioned that he had a toothache. One of the two new lads piped up: “There’s a dopey dentist on Marlboro Street called Joe Power. My family has been going to him for generations. His secretary sends us the bills but we never pay them and he doesn’t even notice. We keep going back to him and he keeps fixing our teeth, free of charge. Check him out first thing in the morning; I’m telling you, Joe Power is your man!” This last line was delivered with a guffaw.

My brother killed the conversation: “That’s my father you’re talking about.”

When I first heard that story, I didn’t know whether to be proud of my father’s generosity or ashamed of his stupidity. Some years later, I found this answer in St. Paul: “If any one among you thinks that he is wise in this age, let him become a fool that he may become wise. For the wisdom of this world is folly with God” (1 Cor 3:18-19). Joe Power the dopey dentist was a wise fool.

Another typical question was, "Daddy, are we rich?" Had he chosen to have a more materialistic lifestyle, the very sons who wanted to know if we were rich would not have existed to ask the question.

The invariable response was, "We're poor in money and rich in love." Some people might consider that corny, and the best of luck to them; I consider it magnificent. I'm pretty sure God does too. St. Teresa of Ávila famously said, "God is supreme Truth; and to be humble is to walk in truth." The second part of the sentence is not so often quoted: "for it is a very great truth, that of ourselves we have no good, but misery and nothingness; and he who does not understand this, walks in falsehood."[25] So, the word *humility* could easily be substituted by the word *poverty*: poverty is to walk in the truth, because the truth is that we are poor, and to be rich is to walk in falsehood. Being rich in money and poor in love tend to go together, as do being poor in money and rich in love.

Back in the days when we nine boys were small children, an elderly lady approached my mother to ask for work as a maid. When my mother asked her how much she would need as a wage, the woman replied,

25. Teresa of Ávila, *The Interior Castle*, trans. John Dalton (London: T. Jones, 1852), VI, ch. 10, no. 7. p.164, www.carmelitemonks.org/Vocation/StTeresa-TheInteriorCastle.pdf.

"Just one meal a day, ma'am, would be plenty." Moved by the woman's poverty and humility, my mother invited her to help out a few mornings every week in exchange for her upkeep. Her name was Nora. The children loved her. She became part of the family.

After my mother's death, my youngest brother wrote to me:

> I remember accompanying her as a seven-year-old on a visit to Nora after she stopped working for us and went back to live in that old cottage in the countryside. Mom had to cut Nora's toenails and clean her feet, which were in an awful state. At one point, she had to pretend she needed to go to the toilet because the smell was so bad she was nearly getting sick, but she didn't want to embarrass Nora.

Any Catholic woman of the time would have done the same. Any Catholic woman of any time would do the same. It's pure gospel:

> You call me Teacher and Lord; and you are right, for so I am. If I then, your Lord and Teacher, have washed your feet, you also ought to wash one another's feet. For I have given you an example, that you also should do just as I have done to you. (Jn 13:13-15)

Persuading children to kneel is easy; teenagers and adults are a tougher proposition, which it's time now to tackle.

Chapter 6
TACTICS FOR TEENAGERS

I. MOM BOMBS

There comes a time in the life of every parent when they realize that, as parents and educators of their children, their hands are now tied. There's nothing more they can do. They find themselves reduced to pure prayer. *Raised* to pure prayer would be a better way of putting it, rather than reduced. Never underestimate the power of tied hands. Christ's hands were tied: "They bound him" (Mt.27:2). Then they were nailed to the Cross. He saved us with nailed hands. You're there with him; he's there with you.

Even in the relationship between Jesus and Mary there is a gradual separation that leads to a greater union. At twelve years of age, he said to her, "Did you not know that I must be in my Father's house?"

(Lk 2:49). At the wedding feast of Cana, he said to her, "O woman, what have you to do with me?" (Jn 2:4). At Calvary their separation produced the greatest reunion of all, and the redemption of all humanity. Mary's heart was enlarged to become mother of all humanity; to be enlarged, it had to be broken. Yours, too.

Parents have the right and even the duty to encourage their children to leave home to make their own way in life. University students should work part-time and contribute economically at home. One year after graduation, maximum, they should be living elsewhere. Christ clearly states, "a man shall leave his father and mother" (Mt 19:5). It's a natural and supernatural law of life. The relativization of the bonds of the flesh is a painful part of human and Christian maturation. Life is separation: separation from places, separation from things, separation from people, separation from one's own body. The only separation that shouldn't ever occur is separation from God. God wants union, not attachment. Detachment leads to greater union.

Your prayer in the painful process of detachment must seek connection with God. A despairing, anguished insistence, a constant, defeatist panic, or a frenzied hand-wringing and "head-wrecking" is not true prayer. Parents also have the right and the duty to remain happy and hopeful and playful as their children hurtle toward hell. It's your best strategy against Satan, who wishes to sterilize you as an apostle by taking away your peace and joy, turning you into an anti-apostolic nervous wreck. Get on with your own life. God avails of these sufferings to purify parents' hearts, to detach them from their own children, to break and enlarge their hearts so that they may give life and love to other spiritual children in God's plan who need them.

It's also true, though, that mothers have more power than they realize, even when their children are teenagers, university students, and young adults. I know a wife and mother who is the only serious Catholic in her family. Her husband is a nonbeliever, the grown-up children are, as the Spanish idiom says, *ni fu ni fa*—neither for nor against, neither one thing nor another; indifferent. One of the sons won a scholarship to study at a university in Italy. During the vacation periods or long weekends, he usually returned home. On one such occasion, the family were seated around the table one Saturday enjoying the evening meal together while this son regaled them with stories about his travels and adventures around Europe: the Leaning Tower of Pisa, the Eiffel

Tower of Paris, and so on. Suddenly, his mother said, "You're throwing your life into the dump."

If you want to know what a "mom bomb" is, look no further. There's your perfect example. She said it with sorrow, not anger. It was a bomb of truth and love to everyone at the table, not just the student at the Italian university; but of course, after an initial shocked silence, he was the first to react, with a tirade of questions and counter-accusations:

> Where did that come from? What's that supposed to mean? What did I say to provoke such a response? Tell me one thing that was wrong in anything I told you about? Do you have something against the Eiffel Tower? What world are you living in? I'm getting good grades, I'm learning a new language; what's your problem?

That's the censored version. It was quite a tantrum.

Eventually, he demanded that she either explain or apologize for what she had said. She confided in me that in that moment she herself didn't fully understand what she had said or why she said it, but she knew somehow that she shouldn't and couldn't apologize for it. So she stuck to her guns, and the boy got up and left the room. Then the others turned on her: "That was over the top. Why did you say that? He was only sharing his news. There was no need to ruin the family meal like that." Not quite knowing what to say, the woman weathered the storm as best she could in silence. Permit me a short, quick digression to explain where she was coming from.

A priest friend of mine, Fr. Jeff Langan, who for many years was a university professor of philosophy and politics, speaks of four categories of university students, all beginning with the letter "s": the scumbags, the sharks, the scholars, and the saints. The scumbags (yes, I know it's a bit crude, sorry), are the party animals who live off mommy and daddy's money and are usually either academically dismissed at the end of the first semester, or dismissed earlier for other reasons. (Jesus was a bit crude too when he spoke about dens of vipers and whitewashed tombs rotten on the inside.)

The sharks are just like the scumbags but they pump themselves up with chemicals ten days before exam time, doing "all-nighters," and pass their exams, keeping themselves under the radar and avoiding expulsion right through the university career cycle. Then they graduate and are unleashed with degrees upon the unsuspecting world. The scholars are those who attend all their classes and spend all their free time in the library. They get good grades. If they happen to be Catholics, they will skip Mass on

Sundays during exam periods to spend more time in the library. They are highly likely to succeed, but they are as unlikely as the sharks to have a positive impact on society. The saints are those who "seek first the kingdom of God." They study hard, seeing it as their Christian vocation, but they do not absolutize their studies. Now we can return to our story.

A few days later, the young man approached his mother when she was alone: "Mom, remember what you said the other day during dinner?"

"Yes."

"Why did you say I'm throwing my life down the dump? What did you mean by that?"

By this time, she had had time to ruminate on the events and had come to the realization that her sentence had a larger context as well as an immediate one. It was not just a response to the mealtime narration of his "innocent" adventures; for some years now, the boy had been flitting haphazardly from flower to flower in life like a tattered butterfly, frivolously "having fun." It was a life without major vices perhaps, but it was without doubt a life without meaning, without substance, without a worthwhile goal. The boy's lifestyle was that of a shark and a scholar and perhaps even a bit of a scumbag, and his mother was impelled to let him know. She answered,

"Because as long as you don't have Jesus in your heart, you're never going to be a man." That right there was another mom bomb. This lady was not for backpedaling. The boy listened, lowered his head, turned, and left the room.

A few more days went by, and once again he found a way to catch her while she was alone, and said to her, "Mom, if you say stuff like that to me again, you're going to lose a son."

Without batting an eye, she replied, "I may lose a son, but you'll never lose your mother." That's three mom bombs in a row. Afterward, she wrote to me: "I can't promise that in some moment in the future it won't happen again. I can't just leave things as they are. It's not me, it's God. I trust that he can do great things with stupid moms. In the meantime, there's nothing left but to pray, offer, hope, ask for strength." Despite his tremendous threat to disown her, the boy's relationship with his mother was utterly unharmed by the entire episode. The seed was planted, communication remained open, and now all is in the hands of the Holy Spirit.

The mom-bomb strategy is far superior to the machine-gun strategy. Mom bombs are deadly and lifegiving. The machine-gun strategy is self-disqualifying. For some reason, a mother's voice can become extremely irritating to a teenager, boy or girl. It pierces their brain like a high-pitched scream, even when it's not. When that happens, it's best to avoid the machine-gun effect of shrill and constant criticism. It makes parents look weak and empowers teenagers in their rebellion.

Mother Mary's counsel comes to mind again in this context: "Do not set your gaze so much on the negative; fix your eyes rather on so many beautiful gifts that my Son is continually presenting to you." In other words, seek something positive to say, even if it's to compliment the jersey he's wearing. A parent's positive feedback is more important to a teenager than parents usually realize. They may not earn it, but they crave it. Find an opportunity. Save the relationship. It's a subject that has surfaced before and will appear again. Prioritize friendship, confidence, communication. Faith needs that foundation.

A school headmistress told me a story about a good teacher on her staff who once entered the teachers' staffroom in a highly agitated state, and proceeded to pace up and down the room repeating, "I must find something to love, I have to find something to love in Dustin McGearty!" The logic of his words seemed to be that, if he failed to find something to love in Dustin McGearty, a pupil who did his best to be entirely unlovable, he had failed as an educator. On the contrary, if he could find something to love, then there was hope that he could educate the boy. There's something in this for parents too.

Shrieking corrections are at best useless and at worst counterproductive. True authority comes from a place of death. That's where the crucified Christ's authority comes from. When mom bombs are delivered from a place of death to self and openness to God, they contain a peace and wisdom and love and performative power that pierce the soul. You must never be discouraged by an initial reaction of rejection. You must know that the initial reaction is a smokescreen; the deep, inner, hidden reaction is what counts. To seek always to have the last word is a big mistake. Seek rather the deepest word, and then let silence do its work. The deepest word is this triple truth: Jesus Christ is the Son of God; he died on a Cross for love of you; one day you will meet him face to Face.

Here is another example of a mom bomb, Irish style. A good friend of mine—perhaps I should say a bad friend of mine, because we were not good for each other at the time—was sunning himself in the back garden of his home on Sunday morning. He was twenty years old at the time. The sun doesn't shine that often in Ireland, and he wanted to get a tan. His father appeared in the garden: "Have you been to Sunday Mass?"

"No."

"Did you go yesterday evening?"

"No."

"Do you intend to go to Mass today?"

"No." The tempo of the conversation intensified with each question and each negative answer, and exploded when my friend stated, "Dad, you know very well that I haven't been going to Sunday Mass for a long time now. I don't go to Mass anymore." His father proceeded to berate him about being a traitor to his God, his country, and his family, when his wife, my friend's mother, arrived on the scene with a basin of wet laundry to hang out to dry on the clothesline. She asked what was going on.

The young man replied, "Dad's giving me a hard time about not going to Mass." The woman turned to her husband and said to him to leave the young fella alone. The young fella was stunned: "Mom's standing up for me, against Dad, about Mass!"

Then came her explanation: "He's a big boy now. He can make his own decisions. We've done our best to raise him right. If he wants to burn his soul forever in hell, it's his own business. Let him off!" With that, his father returned to the house and his mother finished hanging out the clothes and did the same. The boy lay on the rug in his shorts and sunglasses for a while, "blitzed" as he put it when he told me the story, by his mother's words, but the fun had gone out of the sun, he had lost all interest in getting a tan, and he was soon on his feet and off in search of something else to do. His mother's mom bomb had deeply unsettled him, and he needed to distract himself somehow.

My friend didn't go to Mass that day, or the following Sunday, or the Sunday after that, but his mother's words were branded on his soul. They were branded on my soul too, when he told me what had happened. I laughed out loud and so did he, but beneath the laughter, a seed was sown that eventually bore fruit. That man is now a devout Catholic husband and father. His mother's words, in a context related to Sunday Mass attendance, when you think about it, were not that different to the words of Christ: "Truly, truly, I say to you, unless you eat the flesh of the Son of Man and drink his blood, you have no life in you" (Jn 6:53). Therefore, the direct approach has the seal of divine approval.

II. A MINOR APOSTOLIC VICTORY

It's advisable to avoid sanitized euphemisms; not just with young people, but with everyone. A certain crudeness is sometimes called for. We should disregard the ten commandments of political correctness, one of which is, "Thou shalt not raise thy voice." Christ raised his voice. The Gospel tells us so: "He called out, 'He who has ears to hear, let him hear'" (Lk 8:8). He was sometimes vigorous even to the point of crudeness in communication. Especially in the English-speaking world, in my experience, the repression of emotion is seen as a proof of virtue. It's not, at least not always. Permit me to share with you an account of a minor apostolic victory, a mini-miracle of grace that the Holy Spirit longs to perform a lot more often. It has to do with persuading people to kneel.

The religion teacher at a Catholic school in Spain invited me to give an Advent talk to a group of 160 seventeen-year-old students in the school chapel. He informed me that the school was Catholic in name only, and that the pupils knew little or nothing about the Faith. Celebrating Mass for them was out of the question: they didn't know any of the responses, and the priest must concentrate on the Mass, with the result that he could do little or nothing to engage the students. They would then get bored and distracted and start to talk with each other. He also informed me that one of the teachers who would accompany the students was a publicly professed atheist, and the other was a publicly professed practicing homosexual. The third was a catechist in her local parish. He himself, the religion teacher, would also be there.

At the agreed hour, the students trooped into the chapel and proceeded to occupy the benches, accompanied by their supervising teachers. There was a murmur of conversation, no one genuflected—not one, teenager or adult—and they glanced inquisitively at the man in the black cassock at the top of the room. This was going to be fun. In fact, I was at the bottom of the room, not the top: the chapel floor was slanted downward from back to front, so that the altar was below those in the back row, not above them. They weren't looking upward at the altar, they looked downward at it. It was built in the 1970s. It created an amphitheater effect, a bit like the Roman Colosseum, and the gladiator was me. To get them to kneel before God, I had to knock them off their perch. As usual, I begged the Holy Spirit and Mama Mary for help.

The steps leading up to the altar were adorned with the scene of Bethlehem: the stable in the center and the surrounding area populated by ducks, cows, sheep, and shepherds, with the three wise men far off to the right seated on their camels and setting off on their long journey, guided by the star that hung from the altar over the stable and the empty manger on which the Child Jesus would be placed on Christmas Day.

So, I began by asking them what they thought of the scene of Bethlehem. Did they like it? Wasn't it pretty? No answer. I didn't expect an answer. To be honest, I didn't want an answer. I wanted to muse aloud for them to hear:

> But you all are too old for this now, right? This stuff is just for kids. I mean, it's very well done, it really is. It's a beautiful decoration, but it says nothing to you guys, because you're too old now for that stuff. You guys are sophisticated. You know that this is just a children's fairytale. The hard truth of life is that you're born, you grow up, you grow old, you die, they stick you in a hole in the ground, and that's it. The worms have the last word. Right?

At this point, at least I had their attention. A well-known Spanish Catholic filmmaker has this motto: *Prohibido aburrir*. It's not easy to translate, but it means "forbidden to bore." Christ is anything but boring. If teenagers find Christ boring, sometimes it's their fault, that's true, but not always. It's never Christ's fault. Sometimes it's our fault.

You're just a lump of flesh with eyes, food for the worms. And your grandmother too, right? And your mother. Your mother is just a lump of flesh with eyes too, and if she were to die, they throw her in a hole in the ground with a bit of pomp and ceremony, but at the end of the day, she's just food for the worms, same as your grandmother, same as you, same as everyone.

This is getting personal. It's starting to hurt. I know. Bear with me. The alternatives are very stark. That's how it is.

> So, tell me: why do you get out of bed in the morning? Why do you go to school? Why do you study? To get good grades? For what? To go to university? For what? To get a decent job and make good money? For what? Well, let's take the most noble hypothesis: to fall in love and get married and have children, right? But for what? So that your children become food for worms? Is that it? What are you—a living, walking, breathing factory for feeding worms? That's as far as it goes? That's as good as it gets? That's what gets you out of bed in the morning? Ladies, if that's your boyfriend's philosophy of life, don't be surprised if he treats you like a lump of flesh with eyes. Chances are he's going to be more interested in your flesh than in your eyes.

It's pure logic: if death is stronger than love, life is meaningless. The worms or Christ: those are the options. We should satirize atheism more often.

It's an easy, stupid target. Once the wretchedness of the atheistic option has been exposed, the way is opened to return to the scene of Bethlehem. Into this unredeemed desert of hopelessness and meaninglessness a Child was born who would say, "I am the resurrection and the life; he who believes in me, though he die, yet shall he live" (Jn 11:25).

The Gospel of St. Matthew (see Mt 2:1-12) presents three attitudes toward the Child of Bethlehem: those who seek him to put him to death, those who refuse to seek, and those who seek him to give meaning to their lives. Herod represents those who fight to erase the name of Christ from the face of the earth and from the hearts of children and the youth. The scribes who were consulted about where the King would be born knew the answer from the Scriptures—Bethlehem—but they didn't move, they stayed where they were. There are no scribes around the crib. They represent those who know the theory but fail to live it. Then there are the seekers, who leave their creature comforts and pack their camels as lightly as possible for the long journey and set off in search, looking upward.

At this point, I exposed the Blessed Sacrament on the altar. There was no need to ask anyone to be quiet and attentive. The gospel and the Holy Spirit already had their attention. I told them that I was not there to ask them to be believers. All I asked was that they be seekers, that they not live according to fashionable, cynical slogans, that they scorn the facile death-dealing lie and seek out the tough life-giving truth. St. Matthew tells us that the wise men, on reaching Bethlehem, looked downward: "When they saw the star, they rejoiced exceedingly with great joy; going into the house they saw the child with Mary his mother, and they fell down and worshiped him" (Mt 2:10-11). As a gesture demonstrating the sincerity of their seeking spirit, I asked the young people to spend just five minutes now, in silence, in absolute prayerful silence, kneeling, and saying, "Your face I seek, oh Lord, hide not your face; your heart I seek, oh Lord, hide not your heart; my soul thirsts for the living God."

To my relieved and joyful surprise, every single person but one in that chapel knelt in silence: the 160 seventeen-year-olds, and the atheist, and the homosexual. The only person who refused to kneel was the upstanding catechist who whispered loudly to my teacher friend: "I'm not kneeling for anyone!"

He responded softly, "OK, OK, it's OK, stay standing, no problem, let's not distract the students."

III. APOSTLES OF THE YOUTH

Very often, in apostolic work with young people, one finds that the first and worst obstacles are the "guardians of the youth," by whom I mean, sadly—not always, but all too often—some parents, teachers, and even priests. As the Spanish say, they're as mean as the gardener's dog: they don't want any of the fruit and vegetables for themselves, but they won't let anyone else have them either. They won't preach the Good News of Christ, but they won't let anyone else do it either. They won't feed young people's souls with the saving Truth, but they won't let anyone else do it either. I repeat that the school I just talked about was Catholic.

Those who refuse to kneel before the God who kneels before them are self-disqualified as Christian educators. They have no sense of the sacred. To kneel before God is to express awareness of being in the presence of greatness. To achieve a complete humanity, we must learn to kneel again before the God who knelt before us and before our neighbor, to wash his feet, to ask for forgiveness, and to forgive, because the act of forgiving also requires a bending of the knee, the will, the intelligence, and the heart. Modern education does not countenance this. On the contrary, it often militates against genuine education.

If you can succeed in getting past the upstanding guardians of the youth, working with the youth themselves is the easy part. When it comes to sharing Christ's gospel, they are usually a joy to deal with.

"Gentle Jesus, sweet and mild, look upon your little child" is all very well in very specific instances, but for rough teenagers, it's a bit of a turn-off. Jesus "Mister Nice Guy" won't wash. "Be nice to one another, as I have been nice to you"—he didn't say that. Young people have the right to be confronted, provoked, made to think. It's a form of respect. It's what Jesus did. It's what my parents Joe and Mary did too. They were more than guardians; they were apostles.

Early on, the response to their children's apostasy was hard-hitting. To one of his sons, Joe wrote: "Your soul is choking in the fumes of cohabitation." That was a dad bomb.

It elicited the response, "Dad, I fear for our relationship if you keep writing to me in those terms; please stop." He did, he stopped; the Faith was lost, but the relationship was saved.

And so it went with the others: one a busker in Manhattan, two emigrants to Australia, three to London, another cursed by early success and wealth, and others, who after some adventures abroad, returned home and settled into the prevailing Irish agnostic and materialistic lifestyle. Meanwhile, Joe and Mary, silenced but undeterred, resorted to the powerful prayer of tied hands.

And then, year after year, one after another, the prodigal sons returned home, not just home to Ireland but also home to Rome. The Manhattan busker was transformed by an encounter with St. Teresa of Calcutta—in Calcutta. Another was brought to his knees and to God when his wife was diagnosed with cancer at the age of thirty, two days after their wedding. There followed a two-and-a-half-year Calvary which brought out the best in husband and wife. Her priest uncle brought her Communion every day. She died praying the Rosary. Later, her husband, my brother, told another brother, who told me, that his main motivation in life now is to get to heaven to see his beloved Martina again.

My father had a famous poem by Myra Welch called "A Touch of the Master's Hand" hanging on the wall in the waiting room of his dental surgery:

> 'Twas battered and scarred, and the auctioneer
> Thought it scarcely worth his while
>
> To waste much time on the old violin,
> *But held it up with a smile.*
>
> "What am I bidden, good folks," he cried,
> "Who'll start the bidding for me?"

"A dollar, a dollar. Then two! Only two?
Two dollars, and who'll make it three?"

"Three dollars, once; three dollars, twice;
Going for three . . ." But no,
From the room, far back, a grey-haired man
Came forward and picked up the bow;
Then wiping the dust from the old violin,
And tightening the loosened strings,
He played a melody pure and sweet,
As a caroling angel sings.

The music ceased, and the auctioneer,
With a voice that was quiet and low,
Said: "What am I bid for the old violin?"
And he held it up with the bow.
"A thousand dollars, and who'll make it two?
Two thousand! And who'll make it three?
Three thousand, once; three thousand, twice,
And going and gone," said he.

The people cheered, but some of them cried,
"We do not quite understand.
What changed its worth?" Swift came the reply:
"The touch of the Master's hand."
And many a man with life out of tune,
And battered and scarred with sin,
Is auctioned cheap to the thoughtless crowd
Much like the old violin.

A "mess of pottage," a glass of wine,
A game—and he travels on.

He is "going" once, and "going" twice,
He's "going" and almost "gone."

But the Master comes, and the foolish crowd
Never can quite understand

The worth of a soul and the change that is wrought
By the touch of the Master's hand.[26]

Old Joe used to say that this poem prompted many good conversations with his patients. It now hangs on the waiting room wall of his son's surgery, a dentist in Cork like his dad.

Between mom bombs and Nathanic moments, in answer to the prayers of Joe and Mary, the Divine Fisherman reeled in his sons. All but one. Mind you, there are signs that that remaining one was reeled in too, but that's a story for the next and last chapter.

26. Myra Brooks Welch, *The Touch of the Master's Hand*, illus. Greg Newbold (Warren, MI: Gold Leaf Press, 1997).

Chapter 7
CONCLUSION

I. FATHERHOOD AND FREEDOM

Here's a story about something that perhaps a father would be more likely to do than a mother. It's about a little girl named Rosa. Rosa had a special sensitivity to beauty. Even as a child, she had the heart of an artist.

In fact, she grew up to become precisely that, an artist. When she was very little, someone gave her a doll for her birthday. It was a very pretty doll and she loved it. Thereafter, at every opportunity, be it a birthday, or Christmastime, or her first Holy Communion, she asked for a doll. Her father traveled a lot, and brought home a doll for Rosa from every place he visited. As the years went by Rosa's bedroom was filled with exotic dolls of all sizes and colors. Her father was also something of a handyman, and he put nice wooden shelves around the walls of Rosa's room to provide a perch for each doll. The room was like a shrine of dolls. She had one favorite, a blonde doll all the way from Sweden whose beauty outshone all the others.

Rosa became obsessed with her dolls. She spent hours in her room absorbed in dressing them in different outfits and imagining them in palaces and fairytales. It got to the point where Rosa became deaf to the call to the family Rosary every evening. Even when called to the car for Mass on Sundays, she arrived late with a long face, dragging her feet. Her father reasoned with her: "Rosa, you do realize that the dolls are made of rubber and plastic, right? They're not God. God is more important than the dolls. You do know that, right?" Rosa answered with a surly "Yes," as if the question were a stupid one that insulted her intelligence, but nothing changed. Rosa so loved her dolls that she was cut off from her God, her family, and the rest of the world.

One day during the Christmas season, a Roma woman rang the front doorbell. Rosa's father opened the door. The woman was accompanied by a little boy and a little girl who appeared not to have seen soap and water for some time. She asked for alms. The man got some food for them from the kitchen and put it in a bag. As he returned to the door, he suddenly had an idea. He said to them, "Follow me."

He led them to Rosa's room. Rosa was in there with her dolls. Her father said to the Roma woman's little girl, "Pick a doll." Rosa's heart stopped.

The little girl scanned the shelves right and left, up and down, around the four walls. It didn't take long. Her right arm pointed swiftly to the Swedish doll: "That one." Rosa's heart broke.

Many years later, Rosa's elder brother told me that, on his way home from playing football with his friends that same wet and windy winter evening, he saw his sister's favorite doll in the gutter, rain-soaked and dirty with the head and arms torn off. He hid it so that she wouldn't see it. He never told her. He didn't have the heart. Things were already bad enough.

Funnily enough, though, I have told that story at summer camps with seventy or more eight- to twelve-year-old girls, and when I ask them, "Was that man a good father to his daughter that day, or was he a bad father?" the response is always an immediate and unanimous chorus: "A good father!" Rosa thinks so too. Her father broke her heart that day, but he also broke her chains and set her free.

The Our Father is a portrait of the Father, of fatherhood, of every father. It's also a prayer for freedom. Each of the seven petitions expresses a longing for freedom. Even before the first petition, in the first line, there is a prayer for freedom. The words "Our Father, who art in heaven" lift the heart and gaze to say, "Free me from a fatherless and brotherless life; free me from orphanhood and isolation, from a nomadic, Godless, meaningless journey; free me from a horizontal existence; free me from the void of secularism."

When a father prays the Our Father, he's not praying to himself; he is looking at himself in the mirror, not to admire himself because he's perfect, but to perfect himself and become admirable. Children have the right to look at their father and say, "Give us our daily bread"—"Be our protector and provider; free us from physical and spiritual hunger; free us from orphanhood, from the chains of egotism, from neurosis, and addiction."

With the words "Hallowed be thy name," we say, "Free me from the self-regarding vainglory that leaves me empty."

"Thy kingdom come, thy will be done" is another way of saying, "Free me from the tyranny of my own will, of wanting to control everyone and everything; it torments me, it takes away my peace and the peace of those around me."

"Give us this day our daily bread," is another way of saying, "Free me from the fear of tomorrow, the fever of avarice and the despairing accumulation of false securities; give me a serene confidence in you, my Father and Provider."

"Forgive us our sins" means "Free me from the unbearable burden of guilt; wash away the impurity that makes me sick with myself; restore my innocence and integrity."

"As we forgive others" is another way of saying, "Free me from the vicious frenzy of victimhood and vengefulness, of bitterness and hate."

"Lead us not into temptation" is a recognition of my fragility: "Free me from my weakness, because without you I fall, every time, which leads me to despair; make me strong and full of hope."

"Deliver us from evil" means "Free me from slavery to Satan."

In the celebration of the Eucharist, immediately after the recitation of the Our Father, the priest pursues still further the plea for freedom, united to a plea for peace and hope: "Deliver us, Lord, from every evil, and grant us peace in our day. In your mercy keep us free from sin and protect us from all anxiety as we wait in joyful hope for the coming of our Savior."

The Father is guarantor and facilitator of freedom, and every father should participate in that role. St. Paul too proclaims the liberating spirit of sonship of the Father. “For freedom Christ has set us free” (Gal 5:1), he exhorts, and, “For you did not receive the spirit of slavery to fall back into fear, but you have received the spirit of sonship. When we cry, ‘Abba! Father!’” (Rom 8:15).

God the Father gets a bad rap, because he must ask hard things of us, like he did of Abraham. What kind of a God, what kind of a Father, asks of his creature the sacrifice of his son? And yet there it is, in the first book of the Bible: “Take your son, your only son Isaac, whom you love, and go to the land of Mori′ah, and offer him there as a burnt offering upon one of the mountains of which I shall tell you” (Gn 22:2). There seems to be a cruel insistence: “your son, your only son Isaac, whom you love.” In some manuscripts, the words “of the promise” are added, Isaac being the fulfillment of God’s promise to him that he would have a son.

Abraham’s son Isaac addressed him with the word “father,” and asked, ’Behold, the fire and the wood; but where is the lamb for a burnt offering?’ Abraham said, ‘God will provide himself the lamb for a burnt offering, my son.’ So they went both of them together” (Gn 22:7-8). It’s easy to imagine the commotion provoked in the heart of Abraham. Why then is it so difficult to imagine the heart of the Father as he and the Son "went on together" to Calvary? A young widow once told me that her dying husband's greatest suffering consisted of seeing her suffer. He used to say to her, "It's harder for you than it is for me; to watch and remain is a greater cross than to suffer and leave; if I could, I would change places with you." Their union was such that the greatest suffering of the one who suffered was the suffering of his loved one seeing him suffer.

When the Father, in the episode of the Transfiguration of the Son on Mount Tabor, in preparation for Mount Calvary, says, "This is my beloved Son, with whom I am well pleased; listen to him" (Mt 17:5), it's not just a command, delivered in an imperative tone; it's also an appeal, delivered in a supplicating tone. It's important that we get this right, not only to do justice to the true heart of the slandered Father, but also for our own benefit. The serpent's first lie, to our first parents, may be paraphrased in five words: "The Father doesn't love you" (see Gn 3:1–5). The most fundamental and important truth of the Faith is that God loves you. If we lose that, we lose everything. Once our trust in the Father's love is gone, we become an easy target. A man I know, who had a difficult relationship with his earthly father, heard these words in his heart during prayer: "It was not I who hurt you, but only I can heal you." He understood that it was the Father who had spoken.

So, fatherhood too is about healing and nurturing, liberating and leading toward plenitude. St. Edith Stein gave us a sublime portrait of what a Christian husband and father should look like. These few sentences provide a taste of its riches: "[S]ometimes he will guide and lend a helping hand, at other times find it necessary to yield cautiously, and even occasionally to take preventative or opposing action." He will not always say yes, and he will not always say no. His concern is neither popularity or unpopularity, but growth: "He will aid in the development of the talents and energies of his wife and children. . . . If he has to deal with weaker natures and limited abilities, if he observes a lack of courage and self-confidence, he will try to draw out the hidden talents." His duty is "to see to it that every member is made not only to care for his own individual development but also to consider the others and to practice the self-denial required in the performance of his household duties." His greatest mission is "to lead the entire family in the imitation of Christ and, according to his powers, to further all seeds of grace which are stirring in them." He will fulfill this wondrous task, cultivating the "seeds of grace which are stirring in them," if he has first admitted the sower and his seeds into his own heart: "The more intimate his own union with the Lord, so much the more will he succeed."[27]

The man's forte is justice and freedom; the woman's mercy and refuge. The father's concern is plenitude, the mother's is protection. As the divide between men and women widens, the great Christian synthesis of justice and mercy is lost. The categories of right versus left, conservative versus progressive, don't work for Catholics. More women vote Democrat, more men vote Republican. The virtue of the right is justice. The virtue of the left is compassion. Catholics must have both. The vice of the right is anger. The vice of the left is permissiveness. Catholics must have neither.

A mother without a father is more "smother" than mother (too close), and a father without a mother is more "farther" than father (too far). OK, it's a clumsy attempt to be fancy, sorry, but it makes the point that God made both, father and mother, so that each would complement and learn from the other. To be a good father, the husband needs his wife. To be a good

27. Edith Stein, "The Separate Vocations of Man and Woman," no. 38. Consulted March 14, 2024: www.kolbefoundation.org/gbookswebsite/studentlibrary/greatestbooks/aaabooks/stein/seperatevocations.html.

mother, the wife needs her husband. The children need both. It's not about disqualifying widows and widowers. I have a brother who is a widower. His wife died at the age of thirty-two. He ensures that his daughter has lots of contact with her deceased mother's four living and loving sisters. God provides. It's common sense. For good reason, he has given us a Mother.

II. MOTHERHOOD AND REFUGE

Permit me a Nathanic parable for Protestants and Catholics with complexes about Mary and the Rosary. It's related not to sheep, as in the case of the story Nathan told David, but to monkeys.

One of the many consequences of a disordered lifestyle is that you can't sleep when you should and you can't wake up when you should. There are many moments of boredom between the hours of 10 PM and 3 AM Sometimes we're so bored and lazy that we can't even work up the energy to get up and go to bed. On one such occasion, at the age of about twenty, I was flicking despairingly through the channels in search of something, anything, that might offer meaning, that might make life mildly interesting and worthwhile again. I landed on the National Geographic nature channel.

It wasn't even a nature program. It had to do with a scientific experiment with rhesus monkeys under the direction of a psychologist named Harry Harlow, now a highly controversial figure, as I discovered a long time later. Three infant monkeys were placed in separate cages. There were a couple of metal structures in each of the three cages with branches resembling a tree for the chimps to climb and leap and play on. The first monkey was separated entirely from its mother. It was provided with food and nothing else. The second monkey was also separated from its mother, and provided with food, but a wire contraption covered in cloth was also present in its cage. The third monkey was not separated from its mother. The scientists then studied the results in the way all three monkeys developed.

Lo and behold, the first monkey became a violent, dangerous creature. It raged and screamed and bared its teeth, reaching out through the iron bars of the cage in frenzied hope of doing damage. The second monkey was a timid, frightened creature. Every so often it would nervously approach the cage bars and then turn rapidly to run to the clothed wire apparatus, clinging to it pathetically for comfort. The third monkey was a well-adjusted, normal creature. It was curious and mischievous, making full use of the two tree-like structures to leap from branch to branch, occasionally approaching the bars with a big smile on its face, pouting its lips and making funny noises, before returning to its mother for a feed or a hug and then bounding off again to play. The scientists derived important conclusions about mother deprivation. I thought to myself, "All that money and science and cameras to discover the obvious; they could have just asked me," and went off to bed.

Many, many years later, perhaps another twenty, the memory of that night came back to me, somewhat insistently. I considered it one of the most forgettable moments of my life, and dismissed it as such. Perhaps it was memorable only because it was so empty, so boring, such a waste of time, an experience of what the French call *ennui* at its worst. But the sublime is sometimes hidden in the banal. Suddenly, I realized, I understood. God wished to tell me something: the first monkey was a Protestant; the second was a Catholic who doesn't pray the Rosary; the third was Catholic and Marian. Like I said, it's a Nathanic parable for Protestants.

Before the ecumenists come after me with a lynching rope, please hear me out. Rhesus monkeys need a mother. It's a plain and simple and obvious fact. We didn't need Harry Harlow or anyone else to reveal this to us. Motherless people are damaged, inclined to anger or inhibition, or both. Motherless nations are damaged. The most motherless nations in the West over the past five centuries have also been the most committed to war, like enraged mother-deprived monkeys. Motherly abandonment has psychological and social consequences for the person: moral, intellectual, and spiritual consequences. Motherly abandonment has the very same consequences for entire nations. It's logical.

Fatherlessness also leads to war. It's a dynamic that repeats itself in the history of salvation: fatherly adoption and alliance lead to freedom and prosperity; freedom and prosperity lead to pride and apostasy; pride and apostasy lead to war and humiliation; war and humiliation lead to humility and repentance; humility and repentance lead back to fatherly adoption (see the Book of Hosea), and so on cyclically. Jesus repeatedly warned the people of Israel that rejecting him would provoke destruction, orphanhood, and exile, "And they will not leave one stone upon another in you; because you did not know the time of your visitation" (Lk 19:44).

People need a father and a mother. God knows it. We know it. It's a fact so obvious it shouldn't need to be stated. No amount of theological sophistry or ideological acrobatics can undo it. God knew what he was doing. He knew that humans need a mother. That's why he gave us one, his own. Earthly fathers, no matter how good they become at being fathers, are not enough. We need our heavenly Father. Earthly mothers, no matter how good they become at being mothers, are not enough. We need a heavenly Mother. The best thing an earthly father can do is to put his children in touch with their heavenly Father; the best thing an earthly mother can do is to put her children in touch with their heavenly Mother.

Mary is not an optional extra. She is essential. She is at the very center of the history of salvation from beginning to end. She is in the first pages of the first book of the Bible, in God's prophecy to the serpent: "I will put enmity between you and the woman, and between your offspring and hers; he shall crush your head, and you shall strike his heel" (Gn 3:15). That promise was fulfilled when Satan struck God's heel by crucifying Christ, and Christ, descendent of the woman at the foot of the Cross, crushed his head.

When messengers informed Jesus that his mother and other family members were looking for him, Jesus availed of the opportunity to let us know that all of us could participate in Mary's motherhood: "Here are my mother and my brethren! For whoever does the will of my Father in heaven is my brother, and sister, and mother" (Mt 12:49-50). He opens Mary's maternity to all, as the Our Father opens paternity. Men and women, like Mary and with Mary, can "birth" Christ in souls by doing the Father's will and witnessing to him. The Father's fatherhood is not exclusive. On the contrary, it is expansive; it seeks to share, it desires participants. Similarly, Mary's motherhood is expansive. Through her, he wished to come to us; through her, he wishes us to go to him. Without her, Jesus cannot be birthed in our souls, and we, both men and women, cannot birth Jesus in souls. With her, if we have hearts for the long haul, we can be mothers and fathers of Christ.

III. A HEART FOR THE LONG HAUL

Around the year 2016 my community, Servants of the Home of the Mother, obtained a special permission from Rome to celebrate annually on the second of July a Solemnity in honor of the Perpetual Virginity of Mary with its own special liturgy. We were aided in this endeavor by, among others, Cardinal Julián Herranz, expert in canon law. By the designs of Divine Providence, I was blessed to accompany our Superior General on a visit to Cardinal Herranz to present him with a copy of the Ritual as a gesture of appreciation for his help. He was well into his eighties at the time, with black hair—he shyly assured us that he did not use dye—and a face that fulfilled Christ's imprecation to be as innocent as the dove and as shrewd as the serpent. I thought to myself, here's a man who has seen it all and not been corrupted. He told us a fascinating personal story of darkness and light in which the light eventually triumphs.

Cardinal Herranz was born in the year 1930. At the time of writing he is one of the Church's oldest cardinals at ninety-four years of age. He was six years old when the Spanish Civil War broke out in 1936. His father was working in Madrid at the time as a doctor. He was also an active Catholic. Wisely fearing the worst, he decided to leave Madrid and lay low in his native village, Cañamares, in the province of Cuenca, central Spain, until the storms of war had passed. After all, with its population of approximately 450 people, Cañamares was well under the radar and unlikely to attract much attention from either side. But the storms of war struck Cuenca too, and Cañamares. A drunken troop of Communist militia charged into the town on the Feast of Corpus Christi, making their way straight to the church. The cardinal remarked that from the most tender age his mother had inculcated in his heart a deep devotion to the Virgin Mary. Julián Herranz was six years old.

The six-year-old boy watched as the gang of men desecrated the tabernacle, smashed statues, and then turned their attention to the image of Our Lady, hauling her from the pedestal, tying a rope around her neck, and dragging her outside the church. With his heart in his throat, he followed the diabolical procession that ensued as the men made their way up one street and down another drinking whiskey, singing coarse songs, and shouting blasphemies as they made their way past people's homes. Despite being a small boy at the time, the sights and sounds of the episode were branded in his soul for a lifetime.

The years passed, the war ended, life went on, Julián Herranz entered the seminary, was ordained a priest in the year 1955 at the age of twenty-five, then a bishop in 1990 at the age of sixty, and he became a cardinal in 2003 at the age of seventy-three. Not long afterward, he received a phone call from the parish priest of Cañamares, Cuenca, reminding him that his father was a native of that village, and inviting him to preside at Mass there, that it would be a wonderful boost to the faith of his father's people. At first, the cardinal was inclined to say no, not wishing to make himself the center of attention, but he asked the priest to give him a little time to pray about the matter and promised to return his call. A short time later, he called the priest and agreed to preside at Mass, with the following three conditions: firstly, it would be the Mass of the Feast of Corpus Christi; secondly, he would decide the route of the procession, which would take place before the Mass; and thirdly, the children of the village who had undergone the usual preparation would make their first Holy Communion that day during that Mass. The parish priest agreed.

Almost seventy years after that six-year-old boy followed that demonic parade, the same Julián Herranz, now Cardinal Herranz, led the Eucharistic Procession of Corpus Christi along the very same route, in the very footsteps of those men, holding aloft the Eucharistic Christ in the monstrance and followed by the village faithful. The procession ended with benediction in the parish church followed by the celebration of the Mass, in which the cardinal explained to the people, and the children in the front rows, what he had just done and why. He urged them to love Jesus in the Eucharist, to love Mary as the Mother of God and our Mother, and he pointed out to them that we must be patient, we must persevere with unbreakable faith and hope and love, because the victories of Christ are humble, and elegant, and perhaps most important of all, inexorable.

By way of a final touch, he gave the children their first Holy Communion.

IV. GRACE AND THE GENERATIONS

The story doesn't end there. A friend of mine named Álvaro took the trouble to investigate the action of divine grace and the inexorable victories of Christ throughout four generations in his family, beginning with his father, also named Álvaro, who fought on the anti-Catholic side in the Spanish Civil War. Permit me a rapid summary; it's relevant, I promise. Álvaro Senior was born into a poor family in 1921 and was therefore fifteen years old when the war started. From an early age, he was an avid reader of rabidly anti-Catholic propaganda and became an enthusiastic profaner of churches like those men described by Cardinal Herranz in the story just told. He might not have been a member of the gang that rampaged through Cañamares, and then again, who knows, maybe he was. Even after the Communists surrendered and the war ended, he and a gang of marauding "reds" continued their campaign in small country towns in central Spain until they were caught by Franco's troops and sentenced to six and a half years in prison.

Released from jail and reintegrated into society thanks to a family small-business connection, he met a girl, fell in love, and married. The years went by and no children appeared. After two miscarriages and one stillbirth, at the age of forty, things weren't looking good. Then Álvaro Junior came along, but contracted double pneumonia and looked like he wouldn't last. A Catholic next-door neighbor, an army sergeant on the other side of the ideological divide, suggested prayer. Álvaro Senior answered that he didn't know how to pray but set out that winter's night of torrential rain on a long trek, more like a pilgrimage, to the Church of the Child Jesus, without even understanding why. When he got there, he encountered a priest and told him his little boy was dying and he didn't know how to pray. The priest answered, "Sir, you've prayed more than me today; go home to your family." Álvaro Senior made the long walk back home in the pouring rain with the cry "Don't let him die!" in his heart, to be greeted on arrival by his joyful wife and blooming baby boy in her lap. From that day on, Álvaro Senior was a diehard believer and a zealous Catholic apostle.

The same can't be said for Álvaro Junior. In fact, Álvaro Senior lived to see all three of his sons (two more were born after Álvaro Junior) abandon the Faith; when he died, none of his sons were practicing Catholics. Álvaro Junior's trajectory was different to his father's, though, and so the action of Christ's grace and the manner of the victory was also different. Álvaro Senior grew up in poverty and was beguiled by communism; Álvaro Junior grew up in the '60s and '70s and was beguiled by the Beatles and the Maharashi, marijuana and the hippy culture, but he didn't find the peace these movements promised until he returned to the sacrament of confession.

Álvaro Junior's daughter, Eva, went a step further, joining a New Age commune. She was brought back to faith by an aneurysm that returned her to dependency on her parents and to dependency on her God. In the words of Álvaro's wife, Mari, Eva's mother, "The Lord has given me back my baby girl." And Eva's son, Pablo, was subsequently healed of psychological trauma. Throughout four generations, from father to son, from father to daughter, from mother to son—from great-grandfather to great-grandson—Christ's grace triumphs inexorably with the most diverse responses to the most diverse circumstances.

The common denominator? The Cross and someone's perseverance: "He who endures to the end will be saved" (Mt 24:13), to which we may confidently add, "Whosoever perseveres to the end *will save!*" With Christ, of course. Salvation is sometimes instantaneous, but often it's a long and arduous trek, like Álvaro Senior in the stormy winter night, and we must have a heart for the long haul. It's a message that parents need to hear and believe. I've seen it fulfilled also in my own parents, in my own family.

V. HOPE BESIDE AN OPEN GRAVE

Joe and Mary never threw in the towel. They had hearts for the long haul. They fought for their children. Sometimes they had to fight against their children, in favor of their children. In the end, of the nine, only one remained a nonbeliever. Despite the abyss that always exists between believer and nonbeliever, there was a special bond between him and my father. They spent a lot of time together in his final days on this earth. Joe was eighty-nine years old, about six weeks short of his ninetieth birthday (the quadruple-bypass heart surgery at the age of fifty-six was a resounding success).

A couple of days before his death, the father said to his son, "Son, would you grant an old man his dying wish?" Many years had passed, even decades, since their last conversation about the Faith. Throughout those years, though, love had healed many wounds.

"Sure," my brother replied, "what is it?"

"On your way out, will you pop into the hospital chapel downstairs and say a Hail Mary for my soul?"

His son said, “Of course, Dad, of course,” and he did. (Again, I found out through the family grapevine.) Does this mean conversion? Does it mean salvation? I have no answer to that. Ask Mama Mary. To kneel in prayer before the Mother of God is no small thing. But I do know this: Joe Power was a fisher of his sons' souls to the day of his death and beyond. The victories of grace, remember, are humble and patient and inexorable. This was one of them. There's plenty more where that one came from.

After my mother's funeral Mass on Saturday, the thirteenth of May, 2023, on the Feast of Our Lady of Fatima, my religious community brothers and I arrived at the gravesite in St. Finbarr's Cemetery before everyone else—almost. There was a group of children gathered next to it. I knew none of them. Next thing, a nine-year-old girl pointed at one of the Power names on the gravestone and asked, “Who's that?” She was drawn to the name because it was the same name as her grandfather, one of my elder brothers, who wasn't yet dead. That much she knew. It's also an unusual name in Ireland. So, who could this be, with the same unusual name as her grandad?

I first asked, “Who are you?”—and then quickly realized that wouldn't tell me much, so I changed it to, “What are your parents' names?” Sure enough, she mentioned one of my nieces and I realized who I was dealing with: one of my unknown grandnieces.

So, I answered: "That's your mother's father's father's father, and your mother's father has the same name as him because he was his grandfather, his father's father."

She responded, "Wow," and then, "And who are you?"

I said, "I'm your grandad's brother."

She said, "But I know all my grandad's brothers; how come I don't know you?" I answered that I'd been living in faraway lands for many years. Then people started arriving and that was that, but it left an impression on me, next to my mother's open, waiting grave, a conversation across five generations.

The little girl's questioning was more like the questioning of a philosopher than that of a journalist; it was deeper, there was something special going on. She is unbaptized, an Irish Catholic tradition of countless generations having been broken with her mother, my niece. She is a child of modern Ireland, standing at her great-grandmother's graveside. The famous poem by Pádraig Pearse comes to mind:

I am Ireland:
I am older than the old woman of Beara.

Great my glory:
I who bore Cuchulainn, the brave.

Great my shame:
My own children who sold their mother.

. . .

I am Ireland:
I am lonelier than the old woman of Beara.[28]

(Every one of the leaders of the 1916 Easter Rising asked for and received the sacraments before their death.[29])

So we began our reflections beside a grave with an arrow pointing upward, and end with a little girl standing at a graveside. I see not only my own family but my entire people represented in that little girl of the seeking spirit standing beside the open grave of her great-grandparents, Joe and Mary, who in turn represent a lost Irish Catholic tradition, pointing her finger at the tombstone and

---

28. Pádraig Pearse, "Mise Éire / I am Ireland," trans. Jenny Farrell, www.culturematters.org.uk/index.php/arts/poetry/item/3314-easter-rising-1916-mise-eire-i-am-ireland-by-padraig-pearse.

29. See Piaras Mac Lochlainn, "Last words: Letters and Statements of the Leaders Executed after the Rising at Easter 1916" (Ireland: Office of Public Works, 1990).

asking, “Who is that?” I find hope in that for her and for Ireland. God has a track record of turning slim hopes into resounding triumphs.

I’m confident that Joe and Mary are up there too, on the job, with millions of others like them. Call me a naïve optimist, if you like, but I’m not the one who said, “Ask, and it will be given you; seek, and you will find; knock, and it will be opened to you” (Mt 7:7). God’s victories are humble, elegant, and inexorable. I have a Mother to embrace. They give me heart for the long haul. All I need is to kneel.